Neighboring
with Nature

Managing Editor: Katie Elzer-Peters

Copy Editor: Billie Brownell

Designer: Nathan Bauer

ISBN: 978-0-692-90120-5

Printed in the United States of America

Cover Watercolor by Jerie Artz.

Neighboring
with Nature

Native Herbs For
Purpose and
Pleasure

SUSAN BETZ

DEDICATION

For my grandchildren, Cameron, Sabrina, and Elliott Betz and for Landon Rooney's Grandpa Bobby.

ACKNOWLEDGEMENTS

It is a great pleasure and privilege for me to acknowledge my gardening friends for their support and contributions to my book. It has long been said, "More grows in a garden than a gardener sows" and that is true. Grateful thanks to Jane L. Taylor and E. Barrie Kavasch, knowledgeable and kind plantswomen who have mentored generations of gardeners young and old. I would also like to thank Kathrine Schlosser, Pat Crocker, Theresa Mieseler, Debra Knapke, and my other dear Herb Society of America friends for being there for me and speaking the truth with love. A bouquet of thanks to Jerie Artz and Gudren Wittgen for their wonderful artwork included in this book. My gratitude to Katie Elzer-Peters and her team at The Garden of Words for putting this book together, including Nathan Bauer for his beautiful book design and copyeditor Billie Brownell.

"Flowers always make people better, happier, and more hopeful; they are sunshine, food, and medicine to the soul."
–Luther Burbank

——

Introduction

Chapter 1
Native Plants From a Herbal Perspective: Something for Everyone
Page 5

Chapter 2
Nature's Wisdom
Page 13

Chapter 3
Reading Your Landscape
Page 21

Chapter 4
Neighboring with Nature
Page 35

Chapter 5
21 Native Herbs for Pleasure and Purpose
Page 41

Harvesting Tips & Techniques

Bibliography

Websites

Recommended Books

"Oh the things that happened in that garden! If you never had a garden, you cannot understand, and if you have had a garden, you know it would take a whole book to describe what came to pass there."
– Frances Hodgson Burnett, The Secret Garden

Introduction

Neighboring with Nature is a gardening guide for people eager to foster a closer relationship with their local landscapes by planting gardens designed both for their ecological and aesthetic values.

Our traditional planting and maintenance practices in landscapes and gardens are negatively affecting our natural environment, resulting in an uptick of endangered and invasive species and a decline in pollinator populations and water sources. It is, however, within our power to live on more neighborly terms with nature's natural communities and life support systems. We can cultivate relationships that will lessen our effects and improve those places and processes on behalf of all life on earth.

We have reached the point where our plantings can no longer be just ornamental or edible; we need to explore ways to increase natural areas and enhance biological diversity by connecting neighborhood gardens, yards, and community green spaces. This will reduce habitat fragmentation and provide a safe place for movement of the plants and pollinators that help maintain healthy ecosystems.

Gardening with nature begins with respecting a plant's econicity, which means that every plant has an ecological "address" and place of origin and family relationships. A plant's flowers, structure, and adaptive characteristics have evolved over time in partnership with the soils, flora, and fauna living with them in their native communities.

In addition to looking beautiful, in the natural world plants provide critical ecological functions, and have organized themselves into stable relationships within their local communities. Each plant's growth and lifecycle is fine-tuned to increase its own growth and spread, but because native plants are so interconnected with their surrounding ecological communities, when individual plants flourish, the entire plant community flourishes.

Gardeners frequently remark that native plants are messy, and that they do not have the extra space to devote to natives. Some natives are quite aggressive, but others are easier to contain in the home landscape. In every backyard and beyond there is a spot just waiting for the right neighborly native. With all of the regional native plants available, that spot can easily be filled. Some natives fit perfectly into rock gardens while others make pleasing garden path edgers. Others are perfect for plantings along roadways while some are well behaved enough to grow among the flowers in your beds and borders.

When you view a native plant from a herbal perspective you can envision even more possibilities. The defining characteristics of these plants are their past, present, and future usefulness as tasty teas and beverages, culinary delights, in the home pharmacy, for their edible flowers, aromatherapy, and as decorative and fragrant materials for crafts. Native herbs provide a botanical bonanza! The diversity of native herbs can offer something of interest to satisfy the mind, body, and spirit of every type of person. Along with all those attributes, wherever they grow, native and nonnative herbs contribute to the development of sustainable earth-friendly communities by attracting beneficial insects, birds, and other wildlife.

Gardening with herbs personalizes the people-plant connection. The real beauty of herbs emerges when you get up close and personal with the plants. Knowing where and when to gather herbs involves an intimate connection and first-hand knowledge of each plant's natural lifecycle and reproductive habits. When observing a plant closely you will become acquainted with the various insects and other wildlife that depend on the plant. From groundcover to canopy, herbs have something of value to offer humans and wildlife alike. They provide a venue to explore the past, experience the present, and hope for the future. Everyone needs a daily dose of green, and, ultimately, herbs appeal to each of the five senses, enhancing that daily interaction. I encourage you to ponder your possibilities. For a sustainable future garden, explore native plants from a herbal perspective.

CHAPTER 1

Native Plants From a Herbal Perspective: Something for Everyone

Fresh Start Herbs for purpose & pleasure

Herbs are useful plants found growing the world over. From the earliest recorded histories, they have played a vital role in the health and wellbeing of humankind. They're valued for their flavoring, fragrance, medicinal, industrial, culinary, cosmetic, and symbolic uses. The leaves, fruits, and seeds are the plant parts most commonly used. Every plant has a story to tell and represents the living history of any given locale. Herbs are plants that link culture and tradition across generations. Rewarding and easy to grow, herbs can be used to establish landscapes and gardens compatible with your personal interests, family members' dispositions, and hobbies. Gardening with herbs transcends the boundaries of gender, race, age, and social status. Herb gardeners appreciate and love nonnative herbs too. Bees and butterflies love lavender, thyme, and salvias and depend on annual herbs, such as dill, parsley, fennel, and basil, as host and larval food plants.

Black swallowtail caterpillars feeding on dill

Herb gardeners do not always practice traditional landscaping principles. We tend to start with the plants themselves—both native and nonnative—and their herbal uses when planning a herb garden. Their usefulness in fulfilling a landscape function is often discovered after a period of growing the plants for traditional culinary or medicinal uses. While landscaping and garden designs heavily dependent on trees and shrubs can be static, herb gardens are never static and plants aren't always confined to a particular garden area. Whether tucked in a pot or planted in a plot, the ornamental attributes and aromatic foliage of herbs blend artfully with annuals, biennials, and perennials to create lovely, multifunctional, high-performance landscapes. In a garden of flowers, the whole interest lies in the anticipation of bloom, which unfortunately is gone in a few days. Herbs don't rely on their flowers for show, and yet they are colorful. Plant textures vary from furry to smooth and leaf colors range from bright yellow, green, blue, green, light gray, and dark greens to variegated. The interesting foliage and fragrance of herbs lasts not only from day to day, but from early spring through frost, and the changing seasons allow an even wider range of tints and shades of these prevailing colors.

NATIVE PLANTS AND HERBS

The definition of a native plant tends to be as variable as the nature of individuals using the term. It all depends on who you are talking with and their experiences and perceptions of native and naturalized plant communities. The most widely accepted definition classifies native plants as those species growing in the United States before European settlement. Doug Tallamy states in his book *Bringing Nature Home* that a plant can only function as a "true native while it is interacting with the community that

historically helped shape it," including the soil, water, fauna, and flora. Plant nativity is even more confusing because plants migrate over time to new locations or disappear from regions where they once grew. The Herb Society of America defines native herbs as "chiefly seed-bearing plants—annuals, biennials, and perennials, aromatic or useful shrubs, vines, and trees that grew naturally in this country without the interference, accidental or intentional, of man before European settlement. The defining characteristics of these plants are their usefulness, past or present, for flavoring, medicine, ornament, economic, industrial, or cosmetic purposes."

"Herbs have the charm of quiet persons whose minds are yet charged with wisdom and their personalities endowed with the quality that comes of long and varied human experience. They are easy to grow, kindly and responsive in their attitude towards us. Room given them is never wasted."
–L.B. Wilder

Wherever they grow, herbs both native and nonnative contribute to sustainable earth-friendly communities by attracting beneficial insects, birds, and other wildlife. The native plant communities naturally existing in the fields, woods, meadows, and wetlands across North America represent the original herb gardens tended by Native Americans. Where I live in the northeastern region of the United States, four well-defined seasons produce a diverse palette of spectacular plants and awesome wildlife. Native Americans were experts at reading their local landscapes. Their life revolved around seasonal patterns of movement as they moved from one food source to another, continually modifying their behavior in response to the lifecycles of local plants and animals. Each tribe had its own ways of life, which included distinct beliefs, languages, economic, political, and social systems, as well as medicinal, ecological, and other forms of knowledge unique to their tribal traditions and culture. Traditional ecological knowledge recognizes that plants, like humans, get by with a little help from their friends.

PLANTING THE FUTURE

This plant, curly-top gumweed (*Grindelia squarrosa*), native to the Great Plains, was first noted by the Lewis and Clark expedition on August 17, 1804, in Dakota County, Nebraska. Since then, it has naturalized in dry, sandy, disturbed places and along roadways across northeastern regions of the US. Many gardeners consider this tough plant an invasive weed. Native Americans used curly-top gumweed for a variety of household and sundry purposes. Over time, as our needs change, so do common uses of plants. As such, lists of useful plants and herbs will differ from culture to culture and vary from one generation to the next. Several years ago, professors at the University of Nevada, Reno began working with gumweed and other arid plant species to develop low-cost, environmentally friendly biofuels.

"*The first step to intelligent tinkering is to save all the pieces.*"
–Aldo Leopold

They view gumweed as a valuable resource for future generations. Gumweed: is it a weed or jet fuel? There is still much to learn about native plants and keep in mind, it all depends on who is pondering a plant's possibilities.

NATURALIZED

An estimated 3,500 species of nonnative plants have escaped cultivation in the US. Some are now so widespread that they are mistaken as native. Early settlers carried the roots and seeds of their favorite flowers, herbs, grains, and vegetables to the New World. Many of these plants adapted well to their new homes. They jumped the garden fence and have become naturalized members of native plant communities across America. A naturalized species grows, spreads, and reproduces on its own and has little negative effect on the environment in which it lives. So not all nonnative plants are undesirable; Queen Anne's lace, mullein, and chicory are a few of the plants deliberately brought into this country because of their herbal uses that have naturalized over time.

As the production and use of native plants in the designed landscape become more popular, many are being selectively cultivated to produce different varieties specially chosen for their ornamental appeal to gardeners. "Nativar" is the term coined by plantsman Dr. Allen Armitage to describe the cultivated forms and hybrids of native species. But the big question is, are nativars as valuable to wildlife as wild gene types are? Concerns about nativars seem to fall into two categories: loss of genetic diversity and loss of plant traits and adaptions most valuable to wildlife. In some cases, breeding has led to cultivars that are radically different from their native species, and these plants lack the same ecological benefits as the native species. A good example of this is 'Pink Double Delight', a double-flowered cultivar of purple coneflower (*Echinacea purpurea*). While gardeners fancy this attractive cultivar, pollinators and other wildlife find the plant of little value because it does not produce pollen or seed. Look for cultivars or nativars that maintain the same natural flower shape, berry size (if applicable), and leaf color of the species.

An aggressive plant (like mint or violets) will wander about and quickly grow all over your garden but won't jump from your garden into the vacant lot down the street or take over vast sections of natural areas. One gardener's aggressive plant is another gardener's enthusiastic spreader.

Garlic mustard

An invasive species is legally defined by the US government as one "that is not native to the ecosystem under consideration and whose introduction causes or is likely to cause economic or environmental harm or harm to human health." Invasive plants have the ability to outcompete native species, thereby altering the balance and structure of our natural ecosystems. Garlic mustard is one of the worst invasives and one of the most difficult weeds to control in northeast regions of the US. It was likely introduced by settlers in the early 1800s as a food and medicinal plant. Garlic mustard roots produce a chemical that is toxic to other plants, which helps the plants outcompete natives, and it's also a prolific seed producer.

Garlic Mustard Sauce

2 cups fresh garlic mustard leaves, coarsely chopped

½ cup nut oil or corn oil

1 teaspoon ground dried spicebush berries

In a small bowl, blend all ingredients together thoroughly. Cook in a heavy iron skillet over moderate heat for five minutes or until garlic mustard is limp and warm through. Serve over fish.

Native Harvests, Recipes and Botanicals of the American Indian, Courtesy of E. Barrie Kavasch

CHAPTER 2

Nature's Wisdom

"The wonder and understanding of simple beginnings is the fabric of living and life-skills is the art of human ecology and the balance of sanity."
—Anne Wiseman

Schools and educational tools change according to the times but nature's teaching system never goes out of style. Some lessons are best learned directly from the land itself. A sustainable world surrounds us, and Mother Nature is ready and willing to show us how to do things her way. Knowledge acquired by experience is more personal and becomes more deeply recorded in the memory than reading about abstract concepts. If we look closely, every place on earth can tell us many stories: of geology, of climate change, of the relationships between the plants and animals that have helped shape it, and of the history and the culture of the people who have lived there. Our "sense of place" is established not only by the "place" but by our relationship to it, and is dependent upon our first-hand knowledge of and experience with that place. Native herbs are living green links that connect us with our local landscapes and communities.

Like good friends we take for granted, we often fail to appreciate how plant life native to a particular area contributes to its regional character, natural heritage, and inherent beauty. The diversity of native species that defines the character of a place is also essential to its survival. Native plants clean the air, filter water, moderate the climate, and feed people, birds, insects, and other wildlife. Biodiversity is at the foundation of human society; we survive on the range of products and services that it provides. These include variations in plant communities (habitat), variation of species (such as coreopsis, trillium, geranium, and thousands more), and diversity within members of the same species (the many types of lavender, thyme, or goldenrod, for example).

Mother Nature encourages and values community spirit and depends on local expertise. Native herbs are, by nature, neighborly and multipurpose organisms, each one with its own individual character and curious habits. One species may provide special nutrients needed by neighboring plants while another might have a root system that is beneficial for loosening the soil. Some plants repel insects, while others emit fragrances that attract insects. Native insects and birds rely on indigenous plant species in order to feed, shelter, and raise their young; in return, they assist with plant pollination and seed dispersal. Plants and wildlife naturally work together for the good of their ecological communities. Diversity among and within species ensures stability and productivity of ecosystems. Declining diversity and genetic erosion lead to plants that are less adaptive to the changing climate, have reduced reproductive success, and are more susceptible to diseases and pests. That, in turn, leads to decreased food and shelter for pollinators and all other wildlife, including us.

"Is the exploration of the natural world just a pleasant way to pass the golden hours of childhood or is there something deeper? I am sure that there is something much deeper, something lasting and significant. There is symbolic as well as actual beauty in the migration of the birds, the ebb and flow of the tides, the folded bud ready for the spring. There is something infinitely healing in the repeated refrains of nature—the assurance that dawn comes after night, and spring after winter."

—Rachel Carson, The Sense of Wonder

Over the past fifty years, humans have altered ecosystems more rapidly and extensively than during any other comparable period in documented history but nature is still operating under the same set of rules that worked before humans took over. In 2001, the United Nations commissioned the Millennium Ecosystem Assessment to identify the collective resources and processes supplied by nature from which humankind benefits. The study defined four broad categories of services:

Provisioning Services

Any service that can be extracted from nature and is a benefit to people.

- Clean drinking water
- Food
- Timber
- Wood fuel, natural gas, and other oils
- Plants used for fiber, clothes and other material
- Medicinal plants (78 percent of the top medicines used in the United States come from nature.)

Regulating Services

The benefits provided by ecosystem processes that moderate natural phenomena.

- Moderate global and locale climate
- Detoxify and decompose waste material
- Control of insects and disease
- Erosion and flood control
- Pollination
- Detoxify and cleanse air

Cultural Services

Any non-material benefit that contributes to the development and cultural advancement of people.

- Human health and emotional well-being
- Spiritual
- Outdoor recreation
- Educational and aesthetic value

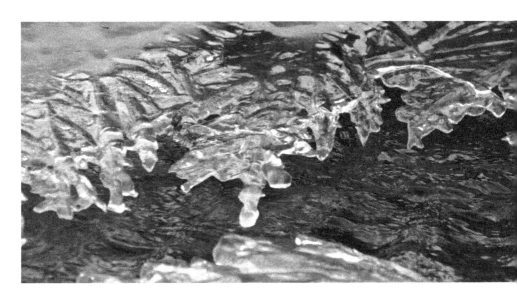

Supporting Services

Ecosystems, themselves, could not be sustained without the consistency of underlying natural processes.

- Photosynthesis
- Nutrient cycling
- Generating and preserving soil and renewing its fertility
- Water cycling

Native Americans believe every rock, flowing river, tree, flower, each glistening star, and every wind that breathes shares the world equally with humans. They historically lived in kinship with their local flora and fauna and viewed these benefits as gifts, not services. Thomas Jefferson, a devoted gardener who took great joy in following the seasons, weather, and dates of blooming flowers, referred to this natural phenomenon as, "The work house of nature." The Herb Society of America's native herb conservation program, GreenBridges™, labels these gifts and services as "green social security" for future generations. Become a good neighbor and start crafting a lifestyle that lessens your impact and improves nature's support systems on behalf of all life on earth.

USE NATURE AS YOUR MODEL

Mother Nature never deletes. Left to her own devices she always completes—she has a plan, purpose, and place for all living organisms. In the natural scheme of things she upcycles everything. The waste product of one system is a valuable supplement in another.

Permaculture garden and landscape design principles teach a holistic approach to living in harmony with nature and creating sustainable human habitats by following nature's patterns and seasonal cycles. Organic gardeners often practice some of these principles. In the natural world, plants and animals establish themselves in reciprocal and stable relationships within their local communities. In this scheme, plants provide critical ecological functions—beauty is a bonus. When the work of one plant is hindered by drought, disease, or other conditions within a diverse multifunctional community, another plant species is likely to flourish and expand its activities. It is this capacity of plant and animal species taking care of one another that allows the ecosystem as a whole to perpetuate itself over time. Here's how you can apply this principle of nature to your own garden.

- Creatively use and respond to change in your garden and landscape
- Catch and store energy
- Make use of native plants and others already adapted to the site
- Use renewable resources and services
- Produce no waste
- Use nature's patterns to design garden details
- Integrate rather than segregate
- Use edges and value the marginal

Founded in 1997 by Scott Pittman and Bill Mollison, the Permaculture Institute USA is a nonprofit organization. Visit the website for more resources, tools and information. http://www.permaculture.org

CHAPTER 3

Reading Your Landscape

Walk around your yard and take an inventory of your landscape and gardens. Observe unique features and key elements already in place. Evaluate and make note of trees—both dead and alive—as well as rocks, wooded sections, and wetland areas. Identify sites that have a potential for habitat enrichment, such as transitional zones between neighboring property lines and community green spaces. More wildlife is found where two habitats overlap than at

the center of either one. Just as humans do, wildlife also have four basic requirements for survival: food, shelter, water, and safe places to raise their young. Thoughtfully plan combinations of these four elements for each species of wildlife you are trying to attract and support.

Let nature be your guide and plant or encourage what naturally wants to grow in your yard and neighborhood. Today, close to eighty percent of the population of the United States lives in vastly fragmented manmade environments with little room for the plants and animals upon which we depend for life. What was once easy passage for native plants to spread and pollinators to move is now an impenetrable maze of buildings, pavement, and monoculture lawns.

"And tis my faith that every flower, enjoys the air it breathes."
–William Wordsworth

Barred owls love dead tree snags

It's important to explore ways to reduce hard spaces and bridge the gaps between nature, your backyard, and adjacent properties. If your neighbor's property has an essential element, such as water, that can be utilized by wildlife visiting your land, you can devote more space to other key habitat elements. Learn to tolerate a bit of untidiness. Leave a few dead tree snags or a bit of leaf litter and keep a few areas bare for ground-nesting bees. Find some places where weeds can grow in borders or patches neighboring your gardens and landscape to provide refuges for natural predators to live and help control harmful pests.

Spiders, caterpillars, beetles, crickets, ladybugs, and toads prefer building their homes and raising their families in the tall grass along the edges of gardens and yards. There are myriad perennial native grasses available in different heights, all with attractive flowerheads. Some are cool-season plants that bloom in early summer; others are warm-season grasses that bloom in late summer and early fall. They're low maintenance, easy to grow, and will provide both food and shelter for an amazing number of beneficial insects and animals.

The seed plumes forming on the grasses in late summer and early fall provide food for winter birds. Birds, butterflies, and small mammals require trees and shrubs of varying heights for cover, nesting, and raising their young.

Another important consideration is to select plants that overlap in flowering and fruiting times so there is a continual source of food

"The landscape changes shape when you start noticing which plants grow where, which plants are good for what. Good-for-nothing backlots turn into fruitful havens. Weeds in the garden look as good as the vegetables. Forest underbrush begins to tell a story as intricate as an illuminated manuscript, once one takes the time to read it."
–Susan Tyler Hitchcock, Gather Ye Wild Things

available all season. Assess your gardens for native plant and pollinators status. Determine where you need flowers to provide nectar and pollen throughout the growing season. Visit the Pollinator Partnership website, type in your zip code, and you can read a planting guide tailored to your ecoregion. http://www. pollinator.org/guides.htm. This site has helpful resources and information, including lists of native pollinator plants for your region, the color of the flowers, when they flower, whether they are a host plant, and the pollinators they attract.

NETWORKING WITH NATURE

Learn to identify and remove invasive species. Plants that are considered invasive in one area of the United States might not be a problem in others. Educate yourself and your neighbors about which plants are invasive in your region, what makes them problems, and the recommended native herbal alternatives available for use in your county. Remove invasive plants that are already on your property. Left where they are, they will spread from your yard to your neighbors' yards and to nearby natural areas and forests. The Plant Conservation Alliance (PCA) maintains a webpage section titled "Weed US: Database of Plants Invading Natural Areas in the United States" to assist gardeners and conservation groups working

Thyme lawn

Home of Roberta Smith

Chaska, Minnnesota Master Gardener

to contain invasive plants in their local communities. You will also find native seed and plant sources, regional landscaping guides, and links to other websites.

Reduce lawn size. Maintaining a lawn utilizes valuable resources, including your time, gasoline, electricity, fertilizer, and water. There are roughly 40 million acres of lawn in the United States, making it one of the largest irrigated crops in our nation, not to mention the loss of genetic diversity and pollinator habitat from widespread use of lawns. It has been estimated that lawn irrigation accounts for 40 to 80 percent of water used in city and suburban environments. There are beautiful native and nonnative herbal alternatives to a traditional lawn that can still be neat and attractive.

Assess the sunlight in your landscape. The amount of direct sunlight that is available each day is a critical factor in plant health.

- Full sun equals more than six hours of direct sunlight a day
- A half day of sunlight equals four to six hours
- Shade equals two to four hours of sunlight a day
- Dense shade equals zero to two hours of sunlight a day

Identify microclimates. These are small pockets in your yard that differ from the dominating landscape in temperature, sun exposure, and moisture. Look for areas of extreme heat, north-facing or south-facing sloped sites, and which areas retain frost and collect snow. Observe wind direction: winter winds blow from the northeast and summer winds come from the southwest.

Learn about and improve your soil. Soils vary enormously from place to place so learn as much as you can about the type of soil you have to be prepared to match your plants to your soil conditions. First, have your soil tested by your local Agricultural Extension office to determine its nutrient content and pH level. A simple way to determine the type of soil you have is to grab a handful and give it a squeeze. If you have sandy soil, it will crumble and won't hold its shape in your hand. If you have clay soil, it will form a sticky lump when you squeeze. Loam, the ideal garden soil, will form a ball that breaks easily when you squeeze it. Author Noel Kingsbury says, "A particularly heavy or light soil should not be seen as a problem but as a guide as to what should be grown."

The health of all soils will always be improved by the addition of compost. Composting is a simple way to improve your soil texture,

"The frog does not drink up the pond in which he lives."
–Native American Proverb

build fertility, and increase water retention capabilities. Some people just dig holes and bury their vegetable scraps in their garden beds and borders; others use compost bins. To find out which method is most appropriate for your lifestyle and the neighborhood where you reside, do some research online. There are many free sources available.

Don't drain the rain. State and local water restrictions are becoming increasingly common in every part of the country. Xeriscaping is the norm in the western regions of the United States where landscapes and gardens are designed using plants with water requirements that correspond to regional rainfall patterns. Mesiscaping, landscaping to reduce water usage in mesic (moderately moist) regions, is equally important for those of us living in the Midwest and northeastern regions of the United States.

Identify:

- High-, medium-, and low-water zones in your landscape and gardens
- Natural water sources
- Eroded areas and low spots
- Build rain gardens or install rain barrels to capture, retain, and control water runoff from hardscapes and buildings. Experiment with native plants to solve specific landscaping problems and water needs.

Each gardening region has its own native species and seasonal timetable. Flowers vary in their bloom times depending on their location; for example, Joe Pye weed might bloom in August in one area and September in another, but plants will generally bloom at the same time in the same place from year to year. Native plants occurring naturally to a geographic region are more likely to possess interesting adaptations to local climate and ecological conditions than artificially pampered plants in overly lush conditions. When gardeners use species that are not naturally adapted to local conditions they are less likely to notice those changes that are purely influenced by season and climate.

"Any one in close sympathy with flower and tree and shrub and has a general acquaintance with nature's moods, could tell the time of year of year without any reference to a calendar."
–*Gertrude Jekyll,* Home and Garden *magazine*

Phenology is the study of the timing of natural periodic events in the plant and animal world influenced by the local environment, especially weather, temperature, seasonal change, and climate. Examples include the first dates of budding and blooming flowers, insects hatching, bird migration, fall color, and the freezing or thawing of lakes and ponds. Observing seasonal events and making connections help people to better appreciate and understand biological diversity. Anyone, regardless of age or education, can observe and enjoy natural cyclical occurrences unfolding daily in their backyards and local communities. Historical records and journals of past seasonal events can be used to help predict future events. Keep a journal recording your planting dates, the arrival of weeds, emerging insects, harvest times, and frost dates. This information can be used to help determine future planting dates, or predict when insects will emerge and pest control should be initiated. Many such correlations are based on the bloom time of common flowering plants. Crabgrass, a creepy plant pest in the

Fresh Start Herbs
Garden border of layered native and non-native herbs

garden, germinates when the soil temperature stabilizes to about 55 degrees at four inches deep, a soil temperature that correlates roughly with the bloom cycle of forsythia. This is important to know if you plan to apply an herbicide to prevent crabgrass seed from germinating. The herbicide has to be applied before the soil temperature is 55 degrees or above.

Understanding insect life stages helps gardeners protect our plants and garden environment. Insects are cold-blooded and their development is closely related to seasonal temperatures. Integrated Pest Management is a combination of common sense and scientific principles used to manage pest and diseases in your garden and home landscape. Monitoring—short- and long-term—is the cornerstone of successful IPM. It is a combination of pest monitoring; use of cultural, biological, and mechanical controls; and reserving the use of chemicals as a last resort.

Place plants together in the right combinations so they grow in cooperation rather than in competition. In this way, the whole garden ecosystem becomes greater than the sum of its parts. Integrate plant species with different sizes, shapes, and colors of blooming flowers to attract a corresponding variety of bees and pollinating insects from early spring through late fall.

Recommended Plant and Seed Sources

The Herb Society of America Native Herb Conservation Committee

Plant Information Online is an on line source to with links to North American seed and nursery firms. It is a free service of the University of Minnesota Libraries. *http://plantinfo.umn.edu*

Plant Delights Nursery, Inc. *www.plantdelights.com*

Prairie Moon Nursery *www.prairiemoon.com*

Richters Herbs *www.richters.com*

American Meadows *www.americanmeadows.com*

Look at your garden spaces from the plants' points of view. Choose local ecotypes and use plants and seeds from reputable local or regional sources derived within your ecoregion. The more you match the source of your plant material to environmental conditions of your planting site, the better plants will grow. By growing plants from seed native to your region, you help support and protect the health of your region's biodiversity. A good place to start obtaining native plants and seeds is through a chapter of your local Native Plant Society. Find your chapter here: http://www.nanps.org

Identify rare and special plant species unique to your community and learn about conservation regulations in place at your state and federal levels ensuring their protection for future generations. NatureServe is a helpful online resource with a database of the number of plant species in each state. By first identifying how many species are in your state, you can then see how many are at risk. This site has good resources for home gardeners who want to neighbor with nature. http://www.natureserve.org

POLLINATORS AND OTHER HELPFUL CREATURES

According to the North American Pollinator Protection Campaign website, eighty percent of all plants depend on pollinators. Pollinators, which are mainly insects, are indispensable partners for an estimated one out of every three mouthfuls of the food, herbs, condiments, and beverages we consume. They are essential for growing the plant fibers used in our clothing and for many of the medicines that keep us healthy. Pollinators are vital members of the delicate web that supports biological diversity in natural ecosystems that daily contribute to our quality of life. The needs of your local and regional pollinators will help guide your plant selections.

Bees

Both managed honeybees and native bees are the primary pollinators in most areas of North America. There are more than 4,000 species of native bees. Bumble bees, leafcutters, orchard mason bees, and carpenter, sweat, and digger bees are just a few species that were living in America long before the arrival of the introduced honeybee. Native bees have strong color preferences and are four times more attracted to native plants than they are to cultivated garden plants. Each species of bee has a different tongue length and favors flowers specific to its anatomy.

Butterflies

Butterflies are nearsighted and like to sip nectar from plants growing in drifts and clusters that give them room to rest and feed. They love red, green, dark pink, purple, and yellow blossoms. Many of the larval host plants butterfly caterpillars require for food are weeds, wildflowers, and native grasses.

Moths

Largely active at night, moths are less brightly colored than butterflies and have feathery antennae. Their antennae act in a way

Adult male
Polyphemus
moth, *Antheraea
polyphemus*

similar to our nose, responding to the scent molecules in the air. The night-blooming flowers that they pollinate are usually light pink, white, or creamy beige and generate a stronger fragrance at night, a strategy meant to attract night-pollinating insects such as moths. Scent is the color of night.

Beetles

These insects primarily pollinate large, strongly scented flowers or clusters of small flowers such as those found on goldenrod. Beetles are considered one of Mother Nature's first pollinator species, with history showing them evolving along with many ancient species such as magnolias.

Flies

Stinky, pale, dull brown, purple, or white flower clusters with easy access to pollen sources are often pollinated by flies. Syrphid flies, often mistaken for bees, are predatory insects as larvae, primarily feeding on aphids before maturing into important pollinators as adults.

Syrphid fly

Hummingbirds

The hummingbird is the number one bird species that aids pollination in North America. They are attracted to brightly colored tubular flowers, especially red blossoms.

Don't forget the rest of the story—pollinator gardens are great, but wildlife habitats do not just include pollinators. There is a delightful and complex world of non-pollinators out there too. It's important to remember the unique roles (as predators and soil builders) that all insects play in sustaining the larger ecosystem. When gardening, you'll want to create enough diversity to attract worms, ladybugs, lacewings, hoverflies, praying mantids, dragonflies, and more.

CHAPTER 4

Neighboring with Nature: Garden Beds, Borders, and Beyond

"A yard doesn't exist in a vacuum. It always has a relationship with the landscape around it, both immediate—that which abuts your property— and more distant—that which makes up the greater landscape in your neighborhood and town."
—Rhiannon Crain

Habitat connectivity is considered the main factor in maintaining biological diversity. Landscapes have different landforms, uses, and vegetation types, and they are loosely comprised of three main elements: patches, corridors, and boundaries.

Patches are defined as a significant natural area that is large enough for a particular species to carry out some part of its lifecycle; how big the patch needs to be depends on the species.

Corridors are linear landscape elements or features that connect habitat patches together. In our natural environment this complex mosaic of plant communities (habitat) provide safe passage for plants, pollinators, people, and other wildlife to move, settle, reproduce, and raise their families. Our traditional landscaping, garden designs, and maintenance practices, while frequently meeting human needs and aesthetics, have greatly diminished these green corridors, patches, and boundaries causing some plant and wildlife species to become threatened and endangered. Bridging the gap between nature, our backyards, and neighborhoods is crucial to the future health and well-being of our planet. We can all participate in the resolution of these issues, in our own gardens, backyards, neighborhoods, and communities. Nature-friendly landscapes are family-friendly landscapes, encouraging self-discovery, optimism, and a sense of wonder about the world in and out of our gardens.

"The design (man) imposes must be constantly modified and sometimes totally transformed by a hand stronger than his own—the hand of nature. Maybe the art of gardening is simply the knowledge of how to hold that hand (the hand of nature) and how to clasp it in friendship."
–B. Nichols

There are a variety of ways to use native herbs in your landscape and gardens, including restoration and habitat gardening. You can also integrate them into your existing gardens and landscape. The first thing to remember is that the land itself dictates how it should be used. Take into account the limits and opportunities of your site and find ways to meet ecological needs of both people and nature. For most gardeners, the best way to get started gardening with native herbs is integrate a few into your existing landscape. Get to know them. Observe how they behave, who their friends are, and how they respond to the changing seasons. Discovering the personal details of a plant's life makes them seem like close friends—it personalizes the people plant connection.

Boundaries are a good place to enlarge existing habitat patches with native trees, shrubs, herbs, and wildflowers. Mixed deciduous hedgerows differ in form and function from hedges, which are densely planted rows of shaped and sheared uniform shrubs. Mixed hedgerows, while composed of plants planted relatively close together, include a diverse variety of seasonally themed trees, shrubs, grasses, and wildflower species. They generally have fewer neighborhood restrictions and are more natural looking than fences. Naturalistic by design, mixed hedgerows offer favorable opportunities for exploring the habits of neighborly native herbs. They are beneficial for creating green connecting corridors for wildlife and increasing biodiversity in urban areas, not to mention their usefulness for controlling wind, pollution, temperature, erosion, noise, and unsightly views.

A "rain garden" is a naturalistic garden planted with native species used to collect and absorb runoff from roofs, lawns, or parking lots that normally rushes into sewers or local waterways. Instead, water is slowly filtered by plants and soil in the garden. Planting a rain garden in your yard or neighborhood will help ensure the health of your local waterways. It will also provide food and shelter for wildlife and add a hardy, low-maintenance, and naturally beautiful garden to the neighborhood. Rain gardens can be designed for any site—shade, sun, wet or dry—and created in all shapes and sizes. Government studies have shown that as much as seventy percent of the pollution in our streams, rivers, and lakes is carried there by stormwater rushing off roofs, sidewalks, paved parking lots, and roads. In the natural environment, soil and plants act as a sponge, absorbing most of the water that falls to ground, creating a natural watershed.

A wide variety of native trees, shrubs, and plants are available in local nurseries and garden catalogs to delight and entice home gardeners. Use the following websites for tips to making a description of your site. List any questions that come to mind, so you will be better prepared to wisely make plant selections when visiting plant nurseries or ordering from websites.

The GreenBridges™ Initiative, The Herb Society of America

A program for gardeners interested in native herb conservation and ways to incorporate native herbs into their yards and neighborhoods. Reputable sources for native herbs unique to your region.

www.herbsociety.org

Habitat Network

Developed by Cornell Lab and powered by YardMap, Habitat Network is a citizen science project designed to help you work together with your neighbors to create nature-friendly regional landscapes. One of the best citizen science projects in the United States. Extensive ecoregion planting references and resources.

www.yardmap.org or help@habitat.network

The Herb Society of America GreenBridges member Mitzi Kowal's garden in Woodbury, New Jersey

Sit Long-Talk
Much

Herbs, Ponder
the Possibilities

CHAPTER 5

21 Native Herbs for Pleasure and Purpose

"One plant in a tin can may be a more helpful and inspiring garden to some mind than a whole acre of lawn and flowers may be to another. It depends on the temperament of the person."
—L. H. Bailey

Most of us learn to garden one plant at a time. The following native herbs are common to the northeastern regions of the United States and all lend themselves to a variety of tactile experiences, such as unusual adaptations attractive to birds, pollinators, and other wildlife. All of them are associated with fun folklore and historical uses by people. Some can be used for activities that appeal to the five senses. They are all easy to cultivate in home gardens.

I have provided their cultural requirements, bloom time, color, how tall they get, and other distinctive physical characteristics. At the back of the book are listed additional resources for finding more information about growing these plants.

When you cook with herbs, you don't just toss different kinds of herbs together because you like each one of them. How they blend and balance together affect the final flavor and appeal of an artfully prepared dish. This same principle applies to successfully growing and using native plants in your home and landscape.

Place plants together in the right combinations so they grow in cooperation rather than in competition. We all have different ways of relating, understanding, and classifying plants. Ecologists use the words "plant associations" to describe the natural relationships between plants; I use the phrase "Plant Pals" to describe my recommendations for a few of the many native plants that will grow with and complement the native herbs listed in this little book. Happy gardening!

"Too often gardeners think of foliage as just being 'green.' When you start to look around and realize how many different greens there are, you will find a whole new fascinating world of beauty and adventure."
–Grant and Grant

Wild Ginger

Asarum canadense

Wild ginger is a herbaceous, low-growing, deciduous woodland perennial. Its large, green, heart-shaped leaves generate from fleshy branching rhizomes growing in tidy spreading colonies. Inconspicuous reddish, cup-shaped flowers droop underneath the pretty foliage near the base of the plant. This is a super summer groundcover. It dies back in winter, and springs to life again in April or May.

ADDITIONAL COMMON NAMES:
Canada ginger, Indian ginger

NATIVE RANGE:
North America east of the Great Plains

HEIGHT:
6 to 8 inches

SPREAD:
1 to 4 feet

HARDINESS ZONES:
3 to 7

BLOOM TIME:
April to June

Natural Habitat and Cultivation

A slow-growing plant that does best planted in light to full shade in humus-rich, well-drained but moist soil. Plants can be easily divided in early spring or fall to increase stock. It's low maintenance once established, but does appreciate an occasional spring or fall application of leaf mulch.

Plant wild ginger as a groundcover for tough, shaded sites or use in rock gardens and wildlife gardens. It is also attractive planted beneath trees and shrubs or in front of taller flowering plants in naturalistic borders and herbal hedgerows. Plant for erosion control. It is deer-resistent. Once established, this hardy groundcover helps prevent nonnative species such as garlic mustard from spreading and taking over a habitat.

Plant Pals

Wild ginger is a great plant to use among spring ephemerals that go dormant in summer. Looks good when combined with foamflower, Zig-Zag goldenrod, maidenhair fern, and wild blue phlox.

Special Notes

This plant is not related to the true gingers (*Zingiber*), but gets its name from the fact that the plant's rhizomes have a strong ginger-like fragrance that were used by early American colonists as a ginger substitute. Wild ginger has a long documented history of use by Native Americans for flavoring, medicine, and fragrance. In the language of flowers, ginger represents "pride," attesting to this plant's spicy inner spirit.

Wild Friends

The dull red color and foul scent of wild ginger flowers mimics dead carrion, a strategy used to attract agents of decomposition, such as native flies, beetles, and fungus gnats (which are the plant's pollinators). It begins to flower about the same time the flies, beetles, and fungus gnats emerge from the ground in search of decaying and dead animals on which to feed. The flowers provide shelter and warmth for early emerging insects. Wild ginger is primarily self-pollinated, though ants like to eat the sweet outer coating of wild ginger seed and help disperse the seed. It is the host plant for the Pipevine Swallowtail butterfly.

Bearberry

—

Arctostaphylos uva-ursi

Bearberry is a low-growing, spreading shrub with glossy, leathery green leaves and red shaggy bark-covered branches that grow directly atop soil surfaces. It's a durable evergreen groundcover for sunny, dry locations. Attractive waxy clusters of pink bell-shaped flowers cover the plant from mid spring through early summer. Bright red pea-sized berries and reddish bronze foliage contribute spectacular color and texture to fall and winter landscapes.

ADDITIONAL COMMON NAMES:
fox-berry, brawlins, kinnikinnick, rockberry, and universe vine

NATIVE RANGE:
Extensive range across North America

HEIGHT:
6 to 12 inches

SPREAD:
3 to 4 feet

HARDINESS ZONES:
3 to 7

BLOOM TIME:
April through June

Preferred Habitat and Cultivation

Bearberry likes well-drained sunny sites with sandy, loamy, or rocky soil, but will tolerate some shade. Because this native species has a broad range across North America, it is best to obtain transplants raised from a local nursery or similar climate location to your locale so that plants will be well-adapted to growing conditions where you live. Bearberry can be difficult to get started but it's well worth the effort. Once established, bearberry will tolerate drought, salt, and occasional flooding.

Uses in the Garden and Landscape

As a colorful native herbal groundcover, bearberry has something to offer both humans and wildlife. It's a decorative green drape for retaining walls, raised beds, and terrace gardens. It grows well in sandy dunes, gravelly areas, and on sunny banks but also forms an attractive, functional green carpet beneath and around shrubs and trees. Good for erosion control. Stress-tolerant groundhugger useful for edging garden beds, as well as wildlife plantings and naturalized plantings. Fun plant selection for children's gardens to stimulate interest and curiosity about the relationships between regional flora and fauna.

"In all things of nature there is something marvelous."
–Aristotle

Plant Pals

Bearberry does not appreciate competition so keep newly established plantings free of weeds.

Special Notes

Bearberry's many common names attest to its long and cherished reputation among Native Americans. They used the plant's leaves, berries, and flowers for food and medicine. The entire plant is astringent. The name "kinnikinnick" refers to its historical use in an herbal smoking mixture made by Native Americans. They used the berries to waterproof the interiors of baskets and used the leaves for dyeing and tanning hides. In fall, bears devour significant amounts of the plant's berries before hibernating. Sprigs of the green leaves and red berries can be added to native bouquets and holiday decorations.

Wild Friends

Bearberry is of special value to native bees, especially bumble bees, which are the primary pollinators of this plant. The flowers attract hummingbirds and butterflies. Bearberry is a good winter food source for birds and a host plant for the larvae of Hoary Elfin, Brown Elfin, and Fritillary butterflies.

" *Come forth into the light of things, let nature be your teacher.*"
–Wordsworth

Wild Geranium

—

Geranium maculatum

Wild geranium is a herbaceous perennial with showy, delicate, purplish-pink blooms and large, lovely, lobed leaves. It is a well-behaved groundcover that forms leafy green mounding colonies via underground rhizomes. Its foliage turns a pleasing red shade in fall.

ADDITIONAL COMMON NAMES:
spotted geranium, chocolate flower, cranesbill, and old maid's nightcap

NATIVE RANGE:
Northeastern North America

HEIGHT:
1 to 2 feet

SPREAD:
1 to 2 feet

HARDINESS ZONES:
3 to 8

BLOOM TIME:
April through June

Preferred Habitat and Cultivation

This plant is easy to grow and transplants well in average, medium, well-drained soil in full sun to part shade. Once established, it will adapt to loamy, sandy, or infertile soils and will forgive light spells of drought. Deer-resistant.

A classic harbinger of spring, wild geranium has long been a standard in native gardens and naturalistic plantings. It makes a nice addition to lightly shaded fern gardens and woodland slopes but flowers more profusely when planted in sunny locations. This is a great pollinator plant in cottage gardens and low-maintenance landscapes, and it's an attractive edging plant in shady perennial borders or herbal hedges.

Plant Pals

Solomon's seal, ferns, celandine poppy, sedges, trillium, columbine, and woodland phlox

"What diversity of leaf form and structure we meet daily and yet how very little does the wisest man of science understand of the reasons underlying such marvelous adaptability."
–N. Blanchan

Special Notes

The folk name "cranesbill" refers to the distinctive shape of the seedpod, which looks similar to a crane's head and beak. In his book *Seeds, Their Place in Life and Legend*, author Vernon Quinn describes wild geranium seed's curious habits. When the flower petals have fallen, "the little head and bill of a bird" remain. Five little seeds are the head; they encircle and are attached to the base of the bill. When they are ripe the outer covering of the bill splits into five elastic bands, and each hurls out and upward, sending a seed flying through the air. Once seeds have landed, they begin to move. Dew or rain causes the seed to curve up. Drying flattens it out, and the seed creeps along the ground like an inchworm. Eventually it will become buried in the ground when it becomes stuck in a small hole or crack. The seed tail's twisting motion helps to push the seed into the soil.

Wild Friends

Native bees, especially bumble bees, and syrphid flies, are all attracted to the early-blooming spring flowers for nectar and pollen. Wild geranium also hosts the caterpillars of several moth species. Chipmunks and birds feed on the seeds. It is listed as one of Douglas Tallamy's "best bets" for pollinators, as it supports twenty-four butterfly and moth species.

Bloodroot

Sanguinaria canadensis

Bloodroot is a herbaceous perennial woodland plant and delightful spring ephemeral. Both the scientific and common names of this plant refer to the orange-red sap contained in the plant's thick underground stems or rhizomes. Fragrant, showy, short-lived white flowers emerge individually from lightly rolled leaves in very early spring while the ground is still cold. Bloodroot is a nonaggressive plant with a mounding or clumping habit. The plant's distinctive rounded green leaves are beautifully veined and can expand to a width of up to nine inches. Sometimes double-flowering plants appear.

ADDITIONAL COMMON NAMES:
tetterwort, Indian paint, snakebite, sweet slumber

NATIVE RANGE:
Eastern North American woodlands

HEIGHT:
1 foot

SPREAD:
6 inches to 1 foot

HARDINESS ZONES:
3 to 9

BLOOM TIME:
March to April

Preferred Habitat and Cultivation

Bloodroot thrives in rich, moist, well-drained soil in shaded locations where protection from the full sun is available. The lovely green leaves remain attractive until late summer, when the plant goes dormant in preparation for the next spring season.

Uses in the Garden and Landscape

A perfect plant for shade gardens and naturalized sites, bloodroot is effective when combined with evergreen plants in gardens where the emphasis is on leaf textures, shapes, and variations of green rather than colorful flowers. Can be planted singly, in drifts or clumps in wildflower gardens, against rock walls, or beneath trees and shrubs.

Plant Pals

Spring ephemerals are wildflowers that begin and end their flowering period during a limited time in early spring when the ground is warm enough for growth and the trees have not leafed out enough to block the vital rays of the sun. Herbaceous non-woody plants, they quickly disappear beneath the natural debris covering the ground after blooming each spring. Spring ephemerals use their leaves to make food through the process of photosynthesis. They promptly store the food away in thick roots, bulbs, or underground stems hidden beneath the soil surface. This food allows spring wild

"Inasmuch as the hive bee is a naturalized foreigner, not a native, the bloodroot probably depended upon the other little bees to fertilize it before her arrival. For ages this bee's small relatives and the flowers they depend upon developed side-by-side, adapting themselves to each others wants. Now along comes an immigrant and profits by their centuries of effort."

–Neltje Blanchan, Nature's Garden, An Aid to Knowledge of our Wild Flowers and Their Insect Visitors flowers like spring beauty, bloodroot, trout lily, and Jack-in-the-pulpit, to jump into action during the first warm days. Christmas fern, wild ginger, bleeding heart, and Dutchman's breeches make good garden companions planted with bloodroot and help cover the ground as it goes dormant.

Special Notes

If you look closely at a patch of bloodroot on a chilly spring day you will notice curious silvery green wrapped bundles poking up from the earth. If you take a closer look at one of those bundles, you will discover a baby bloodroot bud warmly wrapped within its own leaf, protected from the cold and wind. This slowly unfolding leaf is Mother Nature's way of sheltering her courageous prophet of spring. Native Americans mixed the sap from the plant's underground stem with animal fat to make war paint and also dyed baskets and clothing with its red sap. Historically bloodroot was used medicinally and as an insect repellent. It has been selected as The Herb Society of America's 2021 Notable Native Herb of the Year.

Wild Garden Friends

Bumblebees, flies, and beetles feed on bloodroot pollen, but like many native early spring flowers, its flowers do not have nectar. Ants love to carry the tasty seeds back to their nests. They eat the seed's sweet outer covering before discarding seeds in their old tunnels

Violet

Viola sororia

Violets are low-growing herbaceous perennials with attractive heart-shaped leaves and dark purple or white flowers with purple variegations. The flowers and leaves grow directly from underground rhizomes, which form small colonies.

ADDITIONAL COMMON NAMES
common blue violet

NATIVE RANGE
Eastern and central North America

HEIGHT
4 to 6 inches

SPREAD
6 to 8 inches

HARDINESS ZONES
3 to 9

BLOOM TIME
April to July

Preferred Habitat and Cultivation

Violets grow best in sunny or lightly shaded locations with moist to average soils. Many gardeners consider the common blue violet's vigorous growing habit too aggressive, while others value this characteristic and utilize it to solve tough landscape situations. Violets have multiple methods of reproducing, including vegetatively by underground stems or rhizomes, self-seeding, and mutualism! Here's how that works: Ants prize the sweet outer shell of the seeds as treats. They carry them back to their nests, eat the coverings, and help plant the seeds when they discard the seeds in the soil beneath the ground. Both the plant and the ants benefit from this relationship—ants help disperse more than thirty percent of spring-flowering herbaceous plants growing in eastern North America.

Uses in the Garden and Landscape

Violets are low-maintenance, eco-friendly groundcovers for shade and rock gardens. They are nice accent plants for edible landscapes, food forests, naturalized plantings, and cottage and herb gardens. Violets will grow around black walnut trees—whereas many other plants won't. They are deer-resistant and somewhat drought-tolerant.

Plant Pals

Violet's heart-shaped leaves and delicate blooms look best growing in large colonies in front of taller plants such as woodland phlox, dwarf crested iris, and wild columbine.

Special Notes

Violet leaves have long been hailed as a healthy spring green because of their high levels of Vitamin C and A. Wild foragers use the leaves and flowers in salads and spring tonics. Violet flowers are used to make candy, jam, and herbal syrups. Native Americans used violet rhizomes to make an insect-repelling infusion for soaking seed corn prior to planting.

Wild Friends

Violets are the caterpillar host plant for the Great Spangled Fritillary butterfly. Violets are not a highly favored nectar and pollen source for insects, but they sometimes attract native bees and syrphid flies. The plant produces tiny, inconspicuous self-pollinating flowers (cleistogamous flowers) hidden beneath the leaves close to the ground. This type of flower gets its name from two Greek words meaning "closed marriage," and cleistogamous flowers are found in almost all violet species. The *Viola* genus supports twenty-nine butterfly and moth species.

"How cunningly nature hides every wrinkle of her inconceivable antiquity under roses and violets in morning dew."
–Ralph Waldo Emerson

Barren Strawberry

—

Waldsteinia fragarioides

Barren strawberry is a perennial, semi-evergreen, rhizomatous groundcover noted for its glossy green trifoliate foliage that turns an attractive bronzy purple in fall. Cheerful, short-stalked golden flowers light up this useful ornamental plant in April through June.

ADDITIONAL COMMON NAMES
Appalachian strawberry, dry strawberry

NATIVE RANGE
Eastern North America

HEIGHT
4 to 6 inches

SPREAD
12 to 18 inches

HARDINESS ZONES
4 to 8

BLOOM TIME
April to June

Preferred Habitat and Cultivation

Plant in average to rich, slightly acidic soil in full sun to light shade. The plant spreads by runners, forming one- to three-foot-wide dense patches of weed-smothering carpet. Divide clumps in spring to increase your stock of plants. Prefers northern climates with cool summers. Barren strawberry will tolerate dry shade but appreciates a drink of water during long dry spells.

Uses in the Garden and Landscape

Plant this as a functional year-round groundcover under high-branched trees and large-scale deciduous shrubs. It's a good substitute for overused invasive groundcovers. This plant will tolerate light foot traffic. Great plant selection for historical landscapes and Colonial gardens. It is an attractive edging for perennial borders, naturalized plantings, shade gardens, and rock gardens. Deer- and rabbit-resistant.

Plant Pals

White wood asters, bluestem goldenrod, Appalachian sedge, ferns, hellebores, and bergenia.

Special Notes

Barren strawberry's name refers to the plant's strawberry-like foliage and tiny inedible berries. Members of the Native American Iroquois tribe made a poultice from the smashed plants to apply to snake bites.

Wild Friends

This is a butterfly nectar plant and is attractive to native bees. Barren strawberry also provides friendly habitat for toads.

"We have no wealth but the wealth of nature. She shows us only surfaces, but she is a million fathoms deep."
—Ralph Waldo Emerson

Crested Dwarf Iris

—

Iris cristata

Crested iris is a herbaceous perennial with short, narrow, sword-shaped leaves and a bulblike rootstock. The plant's enchanting violet-blue flowers are symmetrically arranged in a series of three sepals, three upright petals, and three showy petaloid styles. Crested iris derives its name from the golden crest along the plant's sepals. It's a very cool plant.

NATIVE RANGE
Northeastern United States

HEIGHT
6 to 9 Inches

SPREAD
15 inches

HARDINESS ZONES
3 to 8

BLOOM TIME
April to May

Preferred Habitat and Cultivation

Plant crested iris in semi-shaded locations with fertile well-drained soil. It will tolerate some sun and average garden soil. Plants benefit from a fall application of bone meal worked into the ground followed by a thin layer of leaf mulch. Divide rhizomes in early fall when its leaves begin to yellow. When correctly established, these plants are self-sustaining and will add years of bright spring bling to your home garden or landscape.

Flower-De-Luce

Beautiful lily, dwelling by still rivers
Or solitary mere,
Or where the sluggish meadow brook delivers
Its waters to the weir!

The burnished dragonfly is thine attendant,
And tilts against the field,
And down the listed sunbeam rides resplendent
With steel blue mail and shield.

–Henry Wadsworth Longfellow

Uses in the Garden and Landscape

Showy spring flowers and attractive spiky leaf blades hold up well throughout summer. Plant along edges or in corners of garden beds and borders. Excellent textural accent plant for shade and rock gardens. Allow plants to spread freely, as the foliage looks just marvelous highlighted by rock backdrops. It's a nice deer-resistant selection for woodland gardens. Drought-tolerant, and useful for naturalizing and erosion control.

Plant Pals

Fire pink, wild ginger, spiderwort, columbine, and violets.

In Greek mythology Iris is a messenger for the goddess Hera and the personification of the rainbow. Legend has it that Hera was so pleased with Iris's work ethic that she created a new flower with the colors of a rainbow and called it by her messenger's name. A decoction of pulverized iris root was used to compound a herbal salve to treat ulcers by Native Americans. A stunning cut flower for spring bouquets, iris symbolizes "my compliments" in the Language of Flowers.

Wild Friends

Blue flowers are said to attract native bumble bees and hummingbirds. The *Iris* genus supports seventeen species of moths and butterflies.

Butterfly Weed

Asclepias tuberosa

An easy-going sun-loving perennial, this bushy plant grows in clumps with upright stems topped by large, cheerful clusters of scarlet-orange flowers. More than seventy species of milkweed can be found growing throughout the US, except in Alaska, and this is one of the more ornamental varieties.

ADDITIONAL COMMON NAMES:
pleurisy-root, orange-root, chigger weed

NATIVE RANGE:
Eastern and southern United States

HEIGHT:
3 feet

SPREAD:
3 feet

HARDINESS ZONES:
3 to 9

BLOOM TIME:
June to August

Preferred Habitat and Cultivation

Plant in average well-drained soil. Butterfly weed thrives in sunny locations but will tolerate light shade. Once established, butterfly weed develops a long taproot and does not take kindly to being transplanted. It is not only drought-tolerant but also dislikes being overwatered.

Uses in the Garden and Landscape

Butterfly weed is striking planted singly or in groups. It is a good choice for xeriscapes, rain gardens, butterfly and wildlife gardens, as an accent plant in cottage gardens, for naturalized plantings, and in perennial borders. In the *Floral Kingdom* published in 1877, Cordelia Harris Turner lamented the fact that butterfly weed was a neglected beauty, but predicted one day it would be extensively cultivated indoors and outdoors.

Plant Pals

Butterfly weed socializes well with other sun-loving natives. Plant with coneflower, black-eyed Susans, goldenrod, asters, fire pink, and yarrow.

Special Notes

Hang to dry or press the lovely orange flowers. Empty dried seedpods of butterfly weed are especially decorative for craft projects and fall arrangements, and cut flowers are gorgeous in fresh arrangements. Native Americans used this plant for medicine and fiber.

According to entomologist Douglas Tallamy, ninety percent of pollinators are specialists, i.e., they feed on a particular group of plants. The milkweed species serve as the only host plant for the larvae of the lovely Monarch butterfly. Milkweed, *A. syriaca*, whorled milkweed, *A. verticillata*, and swamp milkweed, *A. incarnata* are a few other super neighborly native selections for the home garden and landscape. Milkweed is an important part of the ecosystem. It's sensitive to air pollution and is considered a valuable bioindicator of ozone pollution.

In the Language of Flowers, butterfly weed means, "Let me go; stop your pestering habit." Native Americans believed butterfly represented the spirit of childish play and they used images of butterflies to decorate their children's clothes and belongings.

Children were taught to invite butterflies to join in their games. The butterfly game (hide and seek) was one such game. Children would gather a group and draw lots from a specially prepared bundle of sticks of different lengths tied together with basswood fibers. The one who drew the longest stick covered his eyes as the other children ran and hid. After everyone found a place to hide, the seeker would search for them. While he was searching he would chant the butterfly song "Me-e-mem-gwe, me-e-mem-gwe," (butterfly) show me where to go.

Milkweed latex is toxic, and children should be supervised around it.

"Butterflies add another dimension to the garden, for they are like dream flowers, childhood dreams, which have broken loose from their stalks and escaped into the sunshine."
–M. Rothschild

Wild Friends

Showy orange flowers provide a nectar source for many butterflies. The plant's leaves are a favorite food source for Monarch, Grey Hairstreak, and Queen Butterfly caterpillars. Hummingbirds and bees can be observed throughout the summer months hovering, floating, and sipping about this party plant. The milkweed genus supports twelve species of moths and butterflies.

Wild Bergamot

Monarda fistulosa

A true native American herb, wild bergamot is a tall upright perennial that grows in loose spreading clumps of pleasing aromatic foliage. Delightfully fragrant, tubular, lavender-pink flowers bloom throughout summer and form attractive seedheads in fall.

ADDITIONAL COMMON NAMES:
bergamot, square stalk, lavender bee balm, mint leaf

NATIVE RANGE:
North America

HEIGHT:
2 to 4 feet

SPREAD:
2 to 3 feet

HARDINESS ZONES:
3 to 9

BLOOM TIME:
July through early September

Drifts of wild bergamot make it easy for butterflies to nectar

Preferred Habitat and Cultivation

Grow from seeds, cuttings, divisions, or transplants from the nursery. Wild bergamot loves full sun and moist, fertile soil, but will tolerate sunny, dry locations or lightly shaded areas. It's occasionally prone to powdery mildew. The leaves have a minty oregano flavor, so deer tend to avoid them. Plant grows with a spreading habit. You can lift and divide plants when they become crowded.

Uses in the Garden and Landscape

Wild bergamot is an excellent, long-blooming choice for mass plantings or naturalized settings that contribute waves of soft pastel summer color to layered landscape designs. It's a great butterfly nectar plant for cottage gardens and perennial borders. Drought-tolerant once established.

Plant Pals

New England aster, Joe Pye weed, boneset, harebell campanula, coneflower, shrubby St. John's wort, and yarrow.

Special Notes

This species is called wild bergamot due to the similarity of its fragrance to the fruit of the bergamot orange. It was selected as The Herb Society of America's 2013 Notable Native Herb of the Year. Sprinkle the edible flower petals on fruit salads and add to apple

Wild Bergamot Tea

Bergamot, *Monarda didyma*, is the red blossoming bee balm or Oswego tea, and wild bergamot, M. *fistulosa*, is its lilac-colored relative, along with six additional indigenous species of the mint family. The leaves, stems, and blossoms of these choice vigorous herbs may be used in a natural tea for soothing sore throats and settling the stomach. Cover an entire stalk, minus the roots, with 2 quarts of boiling water. Cover the pot and steep for 15 minutes. For an individual cup of tea, use three leaves and follow the same procedure. These herbs are a boost for ordinary teas and contain the anti-septic thymol.

Native Harvests, Recipes and Botanicals of the American Indian, Courtesy E. Barrie Kavasch jelly and fruit cobblers. Bergamots's citrus flavor also blends well with pork dishes. The young leaves are used to brew a mint-flavored tea. It is recommended for use as a folk remedy for bee stings and insect bites. Dried leaves and flowers provide a beautiful, fragrant ingredient in potpourri recipes, and it is fantastic in fresh flower arrangements. In the Language of Flowers, bergamot represents compassion, sympathy, and sweet virtues. Hikers sometimes use the leaves to repel insects. Native Americans historically used this plant to treat colds and headaches.

"An unusual number of plants in our flora bear common names referring to animals, but this is not surprising when we remember that plants and animals are universally associated. The list of plants named for animals supposed to feed on them includes partridgeberry and bee balm."
–W. Clute

Wild Friends

Wild bergamot is the joy of long-tongued bees and is highly prized by hummingbirds. Butterflies are highly attracted to this plant for nectar and caterpillars of several species of moths feed on the foliage. Indigo buntings use the plant's strong, square, hairy stems to build their nests.

Common Mountain Mint

—

Pycnanthemum virginianum

Common mountain mint is an erect, clump-forming herbaceous perennial with pleasing light green, branching, aromatic foliage and flat, modest, white flower clusters speckled with tiny purple dots. Mountain mint is the commonly accepted name for roughly twenty species of *Pycananthemum* natives exclusive to North America.

ADDITIONAL COMMON NAMES:
Virginia mountain mint, narrow leaf mountain mint

NATIVE RANGE:
Eastern United States

HEIGHT:
1 to 3 feet

SPREAD:
1 to 2 feet

HARDINESS ZONES:
4 to 9

BLOOM TIME:
July to September

Preferred Habitat and Cultivation

Common mountain mint is found naturally occurring in areas with moist soil such as along streams, ponds, swamps, and wet meadows. This plant is best grown from nursery plants or root divisions in spring. It does fine in average, well-drained soil in sunny to lightly shaded locations. Once established, it is easily maintained and will appear year after year.

Uses in the Garden and Landscape

Mountain mint's fragrant minty green foliage and pollinator-friendly attributes make this an excellent choice for gardens intended for children or community green spaces. It's useful when planted in front of a wooded area or in openings along a woodland path. Nice addition to lightly shaded perennial borders, cottage gardens, and herb gardens.

It's an effective and valuable plant to deter deer in the garden and home landscape. A few other species suitable for gardens and similar in size and appearance to common mountain mint are *P. muticum* and *P. incanum*. They are easy to find in local garden centers.

Plant Pals

Tall coreopsis, black-eyed Susan, blazing star.

Special Notes

Hikers often rub mountain mint leaves and flowers on clothing to repel chiggers and ticks. Its aromatic leaves and flowers are added to potpourris and moth-deterrent sachets. Native Americans used the buds and flowers to season meat and broth and to make tea. Leaves were used medicinally to treat coughs and fevers and as a stimulant for mental fatigue. Some Native American medicine men believed fresh-cut flowers stuffed into the nose of a person near death would revive them. Mountain mint is aromatic and an attractive filler in fresh or dried flower arrangements. It was selected as The Herb Society of America's 2016 Notable Native of The Year.

Wild Friends

Very popular plant with a host of native pollinators. Bees, wasps, flies, beetles, and butterflies can all be observed nectaring on this plant.

Goldenrod

Solidago spp.

Goldenrod is a herbaceous, stout-stemmed perennial with textured green foliage crowned by bright yellow blooms. Goldenrod flowerheads come in an array of shapes and sizes, including spikes, one-sided wavy plumes, slender and club-shaped wands, or flat-topped clusters shaped like Queen Anne's lace. They readily hybridize, so it's a difficult task to try to sort them all out; only a dedicated botanist could identify each one.

NATIVE RANGE:
North America

HEIGHT:
2 to 6 feet depending on species

SPREAD:
2 to 3 feet

HARDINESS ZONES:
4 to 9

BLOOM TIME:
Species differ in bloom time, ranging from early summer to late fall

Preferred Habitat and Cultivation

When selecting a plant for your garden site, consider its native environment and growth habit. Goldenrod tends to grow in masses or drifts springing from woody rhizomes that spread underground to form colonies or clumps. Plants range from two feet to more than six feet tall. Some gardeners favor the clump-forming varieties, whereas those with more naturalistic gardens can accommodate a more aggressive species. There is a wide selection of cultivars for gardeners looking for more compact plants. Plants do well in the sun or part shade in almost any soil supplied with a moderate amount of moisture. Once established, they are drought-tolerant. Goldenrod is best grown from nursery plants or root divisions set in the spring garden. In spring, control spreading clumps by sectioning off their edges or divide plants every couple of years. Deadhead in fall. Goldenrod is relatively pest- and disease-free except for an occasional bout with rust or powdery mildew.

Goldenrod Tea

These hardy annuals/ perennials were favored by many tribes for both utility and beauty. Collect the fragrant leaves and flowers on a dry day and air dry. Add 2 teaspoons of dried leaves and flowers to a small pot of boiling water; cover and simmer for 15 minutes, strain, and sweeten with honey or maple sap. This is a light smooth tea.

Native Harvests, Recipes and Botanicals of the American Indian, Courtesy E. Barrie Kavasch

Uses in the Garden and Landscape

This seasonal indicator plant reminds gardeners it's time to finish harvesting and prepare for frost. Goldenrod species differ in bloom time, ranging from early summer to late fall. It is a classic choice for gardeners looking for an autumn themed garden plant. Plants can be established singly or in small groups in cottage gardens, rain gardens, perennial borders, herbal hedgerows, and wildlife gardens. Properly placed and planted, most *Solidago* species are easy to grow.

Goldenrod is classified by ecologists as an insectary plant; that is, a flowering plant used to attract insect predators to feed on garden pests. Due to its many valuable attributes, everyone should find a place in their home gardens, neighborhoods, and community green spaces for at least one species of goldenrod.

Regionally Appropriate Selections

Rough-stemmed goldenrod (*Solidago rugosa*): Spreading, clumping growth habit with attractive "wrinkled" leaves on stems that reach up to 4 feet tall. It blooms for three to four weeks in late summer to late fall with spectacular sprays of arching yellow flowers. Plants grow in almost any soil but will thrive in lightly shaded or sunny, moist, well-drained sites. Useful for sunny rain gardens and native herbal hedgerows. A popular cultivar, *S. rugosa* 'Fireworks', is a compact, cascading, clump-forming native cultivar. At maturity, it has a mounded shape that reaches about four to five feet tall in good soil, with arching stems that shoot out in a fashion similar to fireworks.

Early goldenrod (*Solidago juncea*): A low-maintenance, sun-loving goldenrod growing 2 to 4 feet with a 2 to 3 feet wide, spreading habit. Graceful arching yellow flowers and hairless green or reddish stems. Frequently the first goldenrod blooming by midsummer. Performs well in sandy, loamy, sunny sites with moist soil. Will tolerate part-sun and drought conditions. Good choice for a wildlife garden or meadow, perennial borders, roadsides, and restoration projects.

Zig-zag goldenrod (*Solidago flexicaulis*): A woodland plant that thrives in the shade to part shade in dry areas. Its name is derived from the way the stems zig-zag between broad, sharply toothed leaves. Small yellow flowers appear from late summer to early fall in a cluster at the top of the plant. A great selection to use for naturalizing in tough landscape sites and useful for erosion control. Grows up to 3 feet tall and spreads 1 to 2 feet. Can be aggressive. Deer-resistant.

Bluestem or wreath goldenrod (*Solidago caesia*): A woodland goldenrod that grows in full to part shade. Tolerates clay soil. Does well in moist to dry sites. Grows 2 to 3 feet tall and spreads 1 to 2 feet. Makes a nice rock garden plant. Delightful arching wands of golden flowers open from the purplish blue stems in early fall. Drought-tolerant.

Showy goldenrod (*Solidago speciosa*): One of the flashiest of all our native goldenrods. Beautiful, feathery, plumed yellow flowers begin blooming in August and last well into October. Grows 3 to 5 feet tall and spreads 2 to 3 feet wide. Plants grow in almost any soil but will thrive in lightly shaded or sunny, moist, well-drained sites. Drought-tolerant. Good choice for a wildlife garden or meadow, perennial borders, roadsides, and restoration projects.

Plant Pals

Asters, Joe Pye weed, obedient plant, sunflowers, boneset, *Monarda* species, and native grasses.

Special Notes

Solidago, the genus name for goldenrod, comes from the word *solidare* meaning "one that makes whole" attesting to its historical curative uses. Goldenrod's documented herbal household and sundry uses are as numerous as the varieties of the plant. Native Americans used a number of goldenrod species to make preparations to heal wounds, alleviate coughs, and reduce fevers. The juice from goldenrod flowers was mixed with false indigo (*Baptisia australis*) and added to alum to make a lovely green dye. Goldenrod is still recommended for home dyeing. For decorative purposes, the brilliant stalks of goldenrod can be used as cut flowers and are are outstanding in fall arrangements. Goldenrod is unfairly blamed for causing hay fever, but its sticky pollen is carried flower to flower by insects, not the wind. Plants that cause allergies are wind pollinated. The real culprit is the sly, inconspicuous ragweed, (*Ambrosia* spp.) blooming the same time as the showy goldenrods. Selected as The

Herb Society of America's 2017 Notable Native of the Year.

Grows a Weed

More richly here beside our mellow seas
That is the autumn's harbinger and pride,
When fades the cardinal flower, whose red heart bloom;
Glows like a living coal upon the green
Of the midsummer meadows, then how bright,
How deepening bright like mounting flame doth burn,
The Goldenrod upon a thousand hills!
This is the autumn's flower into my soul
A token fresh of beauty and of life,
And life's supreme delight.
–Richard Watson Gilder, An Autumn Meditation

Wild Friends

Stop and look closely at a goldenrod plant, and you will be truly amazed at the activity taking place. In his book *Bringing Nature Home, How You Can Sustain Wildlife with Native Plants*, Douglas W. Tallamy highly encourages gardeners to integrate a patch of goldenrod into their home landscapes or gardens to support insect biodiversity. Goldenrod is the symbol for treasure in wildflower lore, and legend has it that whoever carries the plant will have good luck. Our native pollinators agree, as goldenrod serves as a host plant for at least 115 different species of butterflies and moths, more than any other perennial plant. It is a valuable host plant and late-season source of nectar and pollen for honeybees, bumble bees, butterflies, moths, and flies. Other insects that feed on goldenrods include stinkbugs, lace bugs, treehoppers, crab spiders, and leafhoppers. Native flies and moths lay their eggs in the stems and the leaves of the plants. When the larvae hatch, they stop the plants' natural growth and galls form on the flowerheads or along the stems. One of the best places to find praying mantis cases is on the dead stalks of goldenrod. They prey on the insects foraging on the late-blooming wildflower and then lay their eggs. In winter the downy woodpecker and black-capped chickadee chip open the galls and eat the larvae.

New England Aster

Symphyotrichum novae-angliae

New England aster is a tall, upright, showy herbaceous perennial with gray-green foliage and a clump-forming growth habit. It's one of the most spectacular species of our native North American asters. Magnificent flowerheads of loosely arranged purple to lavender-pink ray flowers with yellow-orange centers. Asters are one of the most abundant perennial fall wildflowers in North America.

ADDITIONAL COMMON NAMES:
starworts, Michaelmas daisy

NATIVE RANGE:
Eastern United States

HEIGHT:
3 to 6 feet

SPREAD:
2 to 3 feet

HARDINESS ZONES:
3 to 8

BLOOM TIME:
Late August to October

Preferred Habitat and Cultivation

New England aster is easy to cultivate from seeds or nursery plants. Grow in full sun or in a location receiving at least four to six hours of direct sunlight. Plants do well in ordinary garden soil that is not too rich. A sunny site where the soil remains moist through the growing season is ideal. New England asters resent cramped spaces and may die out in the center if not periodically divided; limit overcrowding by properly spacing companion plants in garden sites. Cut back plants in spring to control height and promote stronger stems. Water plants at their bases and avoid wetting the foliage to reduce mildew problems.

Europe has no asters at which an American would look twice. In this, our western world, the asters stand all through autumn, shoulder to shoulder in the forest, on prairie, from the Atlantic to California, climbing up to the snows of Shasta, creeping out upon the salt marshes of Delawar(sic)."
–D.C. Peattie

Uses in the Garden and Landscape

Asters are delightful seasonally themed plants, the perfect choice for late summer and fall planting schemes. Use singly or in small groups in the rear of sunny perennial borders. Asters are valuable as butterfly nectar plants in wildlife gardens. They're great for cottage gardens, community gardens, and historical landscapes. Somewhat deer-resistant.

Plant Pals

Goldenrod, swamp milkweed, wild bergamot, coneflowers, Joe Pye weed, native grasses, and sunflowers make good garden companions.

Special Notes

The word *aster* is Latin for "star," descriptive of the starlike form of the aster flower. According to wildflower legend, the aster was created out of stardust after the great flood, when Virgo looked down from heaven and saw the barren earth and wept. Virgil, the great Latin poet, recommended boiling aster leaves in wine and placing them next to ailing bee hives to improve bee health and honey quality. The Shakers used the plant as a beauty aid to clear their complexions. In the Language of Flowers, asters are associated with patience and elegance. So it is not surprising that New England asters are long-lasting and beautiful in fall arrangements as cut flowers.

Wild Friends

This late-season bloomer provides a critical pre-winter food and nectar source for foraging bumble bees, miner bees, carpenter bees, wasps, and 112 moth and butterfly species, especially Monarchs. The dried seedheads serve as a winter food supply for tree sparrows, goldfinches, wild turkeys, and chipmunks.

Black-Eyed Susan

Rudbeckia hirta

A member of the Composite family, also known as the Aster family, our largest family of flowering plants, black-eyed Susan is a biennial or short-lived herbaceous perennial (depending on local growing conditions). The first year, this plant forms a pretty rosette of fuzzy leaves, followed the second year with cheery yellow daisylike flowers with dark brown centers or "eyes." Hence the name black-eyed Susan.

ADDITIONAL COMMON NAMES:
coneflower, golden Jerusalem, poor land daisy

NATIVE RANGE:
Midwestern North America, during the 1800s settlers spread this plant's seed across eastern regions of the US mixed in hay bundles.

HEIGHT:
1 to 2 feet

SPREAD:
1 to 2 feet

HARDINESS ZONES:
3 to 9

BLOOM TIME:
June to July

Preferred Habitat and Cultivation

Rudbeckia species are easy to grow from seeds or nursery plants. Plants grow well in average, well-drained soil in full sun or light shade. Plants tend to become leggy in settings shaded for more than a few hours a day. *Rudbeckia hirta* adapts well to clay soil and will tolerate heat and drought. If allowed to self-sow, this friendly ornamental plant will provide easy-to-move-volunteers to spread around your garden or share with friends each spring.

Uses in the Garden and Landscape

This cheerful, spirited, versatile plant is a good choice for naturalizing on a dry bank planted with other summer wildflowers. Also suited for summer garden beds and perennial borders, wildlife gardens, children's gardens, cottage gardens, deer-resistant plantings, and cutting gardens. Easily grown in containers to provide weeks of color on a deck or patio.

Plant Pals

Mullein, yarrows, butterfly weed, goldenrods, and wild bergamot.

Special Notes

Native Americans used different parts of this plant for a variety of household and sundry uses. A yellow dye can be obtained from the flowers. Dazzling in fresh-cut flower arrangements, *Rudbeckia* represents "justice" in the Language of Flowers. Harvest showy cone-shaped seedheads in fall for dried flower arrangements and craft projects.

Wild Friends

Black-eyed Susan's flowers attract native bees, pollinating flies, beneficial wasps, and seventeen moth and butterfly species are supported by its foliage and flowers. Goldfinches eat the seeds of the dried flowerheads.

Country Maids

Mary laughing Black eyed Susan's
Grow along the dusty way
Homely, wholesome, happy hearted
Little country aid are they.
Fairer sisters shrink and wither,
neath' the hot midsummer sun,
But the sturdy ones will revel till the
Long bright days are done.
Though they lack the roses' sweetness
And the lilys' tender grace,
We are thankful for the brightness of
Each honest glowing face;
For in dry in Barron places, where
No dainty blooms would stay,
Merry laughing black-eyed Susan's
Cheer us on our weary way
–Minnie Curtis Wait

Turtlehead

—

Chelone glabra

Turtlehead is a herbaceous, clump-forming perennial with erect stems and dark, glossy green foliage. The plant's ornamental, snapdragon-like flowers resemble the head of a turtle, hence its common name. Turtlehead is typically noted for its white flowers, but pink-tinged flowers often crop up.

ADDITIONAL COMMON NAMES:
snakehead, shell flower turtlehead, cod head, and balmony

NATIVE RANGE:
Eastern North America

HEIGHT:
1 to 3 feet

SPREAD:
2 to 3 feet

HARDINESS ZONES:
3 to 8

BLOOM TIME:
August to September

Habitat and Cultivation

Turtlehead thrives in full sun or dappled shade in rich moist or boggy sites, but when provided adequate moisture and light this plant will adapt well to a variety of garden locations. Turtlehead is easily propagated via seed, and will readily self-sow from one season to the next. Spring is the optimum time to divide and transplant established plants.

Uses in the Garden and Landscape

Turtlehead is a super accent plant in cottage and wildlife gardens for a showy splash of late summer or early fall color and as a valuable late-season wildlife nectar source. Interplant turtleheads with other moisture-loving species in rain gardens, wildlife plantings, and naturalized borders. The plant's fun "animal" name and interesting ecological adaptations are sure to stimulate curiosity in children of all ages, making it a wonderful plant selection for educational landscape projects and community green spaces.

"The Bumblebee isn't the most glamorous insect around, but the lovable bear of a bee surpasses even the celebrated honeybee in the industriousness department. Bumblebees are often up and out of the hive before dawn, way before the honeybees, and they're frequently still hard at work after the sun has set. In fact, the bumblebee is one of the world's most proficient practitioners of the pollinating arts. Its distinctive striped fur coat is tailor-made for attracting pollen, and the plump pollinator is built like a Mack truck to carry a lot of cargo."
–Janet Marinelli, Bumblebees: The Essential Indefatigable Pollinators

Plant Pals

Combines nicely with asters, cinnamon fern, goldenrods, iris, and obedient plant.

Special Notes

Native Americans harvested different parts of this plant for a variety of medicinal, household, and sundry uses. An infusion of smashed roots was once used as an anti-witchcraft medicine.

Wild Friends

Turtleheads are pollinated almost exclusively by bumble bees. Butterflies and hummingbirds use this plant as a late-season nectar and pollen source. Baltimore Checkerspot butterflies lay their eggs on turtleheads.

A busy bee at work

Spicebush

—

Lindera benzoin

Spicebush is a deciduous woodland understory shrub that commonly grows six to twelve feet tall, but occasionally will reach fifteen feet or more. It's an excellent low-maintenance shrub with multiple season interest. In early spring, fragrant yellow flowers appear before the leaves, bundled along the plant's bare dark brown branches. *Lindera* species have emerald green leaves and fragrant stems that give off a spicy clove scent when crushed or split. Spicebush foliage turns rich golden yellow in autumn, lending a perfect backdrop for the shrub's glowing red berries (drupes). Plants are dioecious, bearing only male or female flowers on each individual shrub. You need to plant a male and a female plant if you want to enjoy the fall fruit show.

ADDITIONAL COMMON NAMES:
wild spice, Benjamin bush, snap wood, fever bush

NATIVE RANGE:
Eastern United States

HEIGHT:
6 to 12 feet

SPREAD:
6 to 12 feet

HARDINESS ZONES:
4 to 9

BLOOM TIME:
April

Preferred Habitat and Cultivation

Propagate plants from softwood cuttings or find nursery plants. Spicebush is easy going and does fine grown in average, medium, well-drained soil in full sun to part shade. Unlike many other shrubs, spicebush will tolerate damp shaded locations. That being said, the best fall color and berries are produced when it's planted in some sun.

Uses in the Garden and Landscape

Spicebush is the perfect companion to shade-loving herbs and is spectacular in group plantings as a hedge or screen rather than as a specimen plant. Useful in naturalized plantings, and an excellent choice for educational landscapes, wildflower gardens, and historical landscapes. Deer-resistant and tolerates drought quite well once established. Designated The Herb Society of America 2012 Notable Native Herb of the Year.

Plant Pals

Bloodroot, wild ginger, Virginia bluebells, beautyberry, wild asters, and Christmas fern.

Special Notes

Native Americans highly valued the berries, stems, and leaves of spicebush for a host of medicinal, household, and sundry uses. Early American settlers used the dried bark in place of cinnamon and allspice, the leaves were used for teas, and the berries were used to flavor meats, soups, sauces, and vegetables. During the Civil War, spicebush tea was substituted for coffee when provisions were sparse. Hikers rub its aromatic leaves on their clothing to perk up their spirits and to repel insects.

Wild Friends

Humans, beneficial insects, butterflies, and songbirds can all utilize this multifunctional herbal shrub. Spicebush's relationship with native North American wildlife dates back centuries as it has furnished safe shelter, nesting sites, and food for various bird species. The red berries' high-fat content provide a valuable source of energy for long-distance migratory birds. It is the favored host and larval plant Eastern Tiger Swallowtail and Spicebush Swallowtail butterfly.

Elderberry

—

Sambucus canadensis

American elder is a small tree or multistemmed shrub with profusely spreading stoloniferous roots that multiply over time to form a thicket. Wild elderberry flourishes in sunny, moist forest clearings, along the damp edges of fields, and next to streams and roadside ditches. The bushes are easy to identify after their fragrant, creamy white, umbel-bearing flowers burst forth in early summer. By summer's end, the flowers are replaced with dense clusters of dark purple edible berries.

ADDITIONAL COMMON NAMES:
wild spice, Benjamin bush, snap wood, fever bush, saskatoon

NATIVE RANGE:
Eastern United States

HEIGHT:
6 to 12 feet

SPREAD:
6 to 12 feet

HARDINESS ZONES:
4 to 9

BLOOM TIME:
April

Preferred Habitat and Cultivation

Elderberry is adaptable and easy to grow in average, medium to wet humus-filled soil in full sun to part shade. Prune out dead or weakened stems in early spring. This can be a high maintenance plant and needs to be properly sited due to its suckering and spreading growth habit.

A multifunctional plant, elderberry can perform a variety of roles in native plantings and wildlife borders. It grows well when planted in drifts at the edges of woods. Organic gardeners plant elderberry bushes along garden edges to protect plants from visiting garden pests, and prepare decoctions from elder leaves to spray garden plants to repel caterpillars and prevent powdery mildew.

Elderberry Ink Recipe

Strainer
Bowl
Small glass jar
½ cup elderberries
½ teaspoon vinegar
½ teaspoon salt

Mash the elderberries through a strainer until you get a pulp-free juice. Add the vinegar and salt to the fresh juice, and mix well. The vinegar helps to hold the color and the salt acts as a preservative. Store is in a glass jar. A small paintbrush works well for writing or drawing pictures.

~ Susan Betz

Special Notes

Nicknamed "the medicine chest of the people," elderberry has been used for food and medicine since ancient times. It is said to have been in cultivation since 1761. In his book *Volunteer Vegetable Sampler*, ethnobotanist Dr. Peter Gail comments, "As food, elderberries are ripe twice each year," referring to when the plants flower and when they produce berries. The flowers and berries are useful for making pies, wines, candies, beverages, jellies, and toiletries; both have strong medicinal properties. Throughout plant folklore, the American elder is traditionally considered the mother and has been credited with having peculiar power to protect all other herbs, allowing them to thrive. People planted elderberry bushes within the corners of their herb gardens close to a house to protect the plants and promote good health for themselves and their families. In times past, many folks refused to cut down or burn an elderberry bush without first asking permission of its guardian. "Old girl give me some of thy wood and I will give you some of mine, when I grow into a tree." Legend states that if one sprinkles elderberry flowers and berries or leaves on a person or place, one can make wishes come true. The Native Americans called elderberry "the tree of music" and made flutes from branches cut and dried in spring. Young boys used to hollow the soft pitch from elderberry shoots to make popguns and whistles. Little girls would smash the berries to produce a lovely purple dye for coloring their doll's clothes. In times past, sniffling children were given sugar pills soaked in a homeopathic elderflower tincture. Wild elder was the International Herb Association 2013 Herb of the year.

Wild Friends

The flowers and berries attract bees, a surprising number of bird species, and other wildlife. Elderberry flowers are not a huge favorite

"When the days have grown in length, when the sun has greater power shinning in his noonday strength. When the Elder tree's in flower; when each shady kind of place. By the stream and up the lane shows its mass of creamy lace—Summer's really come again."

–Cicely M. Baker, Fairies of The Trees

with butterflies, but native bees, flies, and beetles can be observed lunching on the flower pollen. The carpenter bee, a charming creature that's only one-quarter of an inch in length with a shiny blue body and rainbow-tinted wings, uses dead elderberry twigs to construct an "apartment house" for her family in late spring. She searches for the perfect broken elderberry twig and hollows out the pith, creating a tunnel divided into separate "rooms." The walls are formed from bits of elderberry pith glued together with bee saliva. She then gathers pollen and stocks each room with a loaf of beebread and lays her egg upon it. She saves a space in the stem for herself to stay while her family is growing up

Witch Hazel

Hamamelis virginiana

Witch hazel is a deciduous, multistemmed small tree or shrub with a graceful vase-shaped growth habit. The tree's smooth, grayish-brown branches are interestingly forked and twisted and covered with slightly fragrant, oval, dark green leaves that give way to attractive yellow fall color. The bright yellow fall-blooming flowers have long, thin twisted petals with a light pleasant fragrance. Interesting seedpods develop later.

ADDITIONAL COMMON NAMES
spotted alder, snapping hazelnut, and winter bloom

NATIVE RANGE
Eastern North America

HEIGHT
15 to 20 feet

SPREAD
10 to 20 feet

HARDINESS ZONES
3 to 8

BLOOM TIME
October to November

Preferred Habitat and Cultivation

Witch hazel prefers well-drained loamy soils and will tolerate a variety of moisture conditions. Full sun to part shade are the best light conditions for this plant. Once established, witch hazels are easy to maintain and relatively pest- and disease-free.

Witch hazel has some curious habits that set it apart from other trees and shrubs. It is the most inconspicuous tree in the woods during the spring season, but by late fall when all the other trees are preparing for winter, from its thin twisted branches aromatic spidery yellow flowers burst forth. The fruit, which takes a year to mature, is a woody capsule containing two shiny, hard, black seeds. The ripe seed capsules explode, shooting seeds 10 to 30 feet away. This is Mother Nature's way of helping witch hazel's heavy seed find a place to germinate at a distance from the mother plant, thus eliminating competition for soil, nutrients, and moisture. Witch hazels are lovely when planted against the backdrop of dark evergreens, planted along the edges of native hedges or woodlands, and as naturalized borders and wildlife plantings.

Through the gray and somber wood,
Against the dusk of fir and pine
Last of their
floral sisterhood
The hazel's yellow blossoms shine.
–John G. Whittier

Native Americans used the leaves, twigs, and bark to make an astringent tonic to ease external inflammations. Witch hazel water is used to treat insect bites and relieve itching, especially on chigger and tick bites, as well as mosquito bites and poison ivy rash. Witch hazel extracts have been used in skin creams, lotions, and ointments since the 1840s. Witch hazel twigs have long been used as divining rods by "well-witchers" to locate underground water sources before digging water wells. So, it's not surprising that witch hazel represents "a spell" in the Language of Flowers. If you bring a few branches of witch hazel inside in late November, the warmth of

Witch hazel twigs were used as divining rods

the house will "set off" last year's seed capsules, catapulting seeds all over the room. Witch hazel has been selected as the 2020 Herb Society Notable Native Herb Of the Year.

Wild Friends

Within its natural plant community witch hazel is an understory plant that provides nesting sites for various bird species that prefer to build nests in the low, lateral branches of trees and shrubs. Wild turkey and ruffed grouse like to eat the seeds while rabbits and squirrels eat the bark, leaves, and seeds.

Fragrant Sumac

—

Rhus aromatica

Sumacs are small, deciduous, woody trees or shrubs characterized by attractive red seedheads, brilliant scarlet fall leaves, yellowish white spring flowers, and a habit of spreading into thickets by their suckering root systems. Fragrant sumac has glossy blue-green leaves that turn shades of red and burgundy in fall and emit a lemon scent when crushed. "Clouds" of small yellow spring flower clusters ripen into large, red, shiny berries.

ADDITIONAL COMMON NAMES:
lemon sumac, polecat sumac

NATIVE RANGE:
A variety of sumac species can be found growing in clearings, vacant lots, and along roadways throughout the United States and Canada.

HEIGHT:
6 to 8 feet

SPREAD:
6 to 10 feet

HARDINESS ZONES:
3 to 9

BLOOM TIME:
May to June

Preferred Habitat and Cultivation

Tough, adaptable, and easy to grow, sumac flourishes in average, well-drained soil in sun to part shade. Does not tolerant overly damp, poorly drained sites.

Fragrant sumac's spreading roots, dense foliage, and tolerance of dry poor soils make it an excellent plant for erosion control and for stabilizing banks and slopes. Fragrant sumac is an attractive shrub for naturalized landscape plantings where its aggressive personality will not cause problems. Its distinctive foliage and bright red berries make it one of the best ornamentals for mass plantings in butterfly and songbird gardens. Sumac easily adjusts to disturbed sites, is salt-tolerant, and is useful as a transitional plant in environmental rehabilitation.

Indian Lemonade Recipe

The culinary use of native American sumacs is primarily to make a refreshing tart drink, reminiscent of lemonade, and often called "Indian lemonade." The berries of either smooth sumac (*Rhus glabra*) or staghorn sumac (*Rhus typhina*) can be used, the latter is the tarter of the two. Sumac "lemonade" can be made by soaking a stalk of tightly packed red sumac berries in a pitcher of cold water overnight. If you use hot water, you'll get more tannin in your drink. Strain through several layers of cheesecloth to remove the berries and their hairs. Sweeten to taste, and drink. One source says to drink the sumac lemonade right after making it as the flavor changes rapidly. You can also make a hot drink with the berries and flavor it with maple syrup.

–Courtesy Katherine Schosser (GreenBridges™)

Native Americans used fresh sumac berries to brew a refreshing, tart, pink lemonade-like beverage. They used the roots, bark, and leaves in medicinal preparations to cure a variety of ailments. Sumac leaves were also used to brew a brown dye; the roots, a yellow dye, and the inner bark and pith of the stem were mixed with bloodroot to make an orange dye. The bark and stems of the sumac were gathered for basket making. At one time, sumac branches were used as tapping spouts to collect maple sap in spring. Children made whistles and peashooters from the shrub's hollowed stems.

Wild Friends

Songbirds eat the tart, red fall berries, and the plants provide an excellent winter source of food for wildlife. Honeybees and butterflies are attracted to the spring flowers and native carpenter bees build their nest cells in the pithy centers of the tree's branches. Sumac is a host plant for the Red-banded Hairstreak butterfly. Bluebirds, various finches, and robins are especially attracted to sumacs.

Serviceberry

Amelanchier canadensis

Serviceberries are deciduous, flowering, upright multistemmed shrubs or small trees. Charming, dainty fragrant flowers appear early in spring before the leaves have fully emerged. Humans and songbirds both enjoy the tasty, edible, reddish purple summer berries. Dark green summer foliage transitions into an eye-catching fall blend of golden orange or reddish green hues.

ADDITIONAL COMMON NAMES
shadblow, Juneberry

NATIVE RANGE
Eastern North America

HEIGHT
25 to 30 feet

SPREAD
15 to 20 feet

HARDINESS ZONES
3 to 8

BLOOM TIME
April to May

Serviceberries are easily propagated by seeds, cuttings, or nursery starts. Shadblow grows well in full sun or dappled shade and is easily cultivated in well-drained average to medium moist soils. Serviceberry's multiple stems occasionally need pruning if you wish to maintain a trunk shape. Juneberry is drought-tolerant once established, and it will adapt to clay soils.

Indian Pudding

2 cups raisins
2 cups fine cornmeal
4 cups water
½ cup nut butter
½ cup honey
¼ cup Juneberries, fresh or dried
½ teaspoon ground ginger
½ teaspoon nutmeg

Toss raisins and cornmeal together gently. Bring the water to boil with nut butter in large saucepan. Gradually add the cornmeal-raisin mixture and simmer, stirring, until it thickens in about 15 minutes. Add the remaining ingredients, blending thoroughly. Pour into a 2 1/2 quart-sized casserole dish. Set the casserole dish in a pan of water, 1 to 2 inches deep, and bake in a pre-heated 325 degree F oven for 2 1/2 hours. Cool thoroughly before serving. Serve with nut milk or additional nutmeg for topping.

Native Harvests, Recipes and Botanicals of the American Indian– Courtesy E. Barrie Kavasch

Serviceberry is a tremendous multiseasonal native alternative to the 'Bradford' pear or cherry tree in the home landscape. It is a beneficial understory plant sited along the edges of wood-lands and in herbal hedgerows. This is a super low-maintenance tree or shrub for historical landscapes, community green spaces, permaculture or wildlife gardens, and naturalized borders. It's attractive when grown as a specimen tree or grouped as an overflowing, informal hedge.

Special Notes

Serviceberry has been used as a seasonal indicator for thousands of years. Early colonists who settled in wilderness areas far from civilization waited until spring to hold memorial services for loved ones who had passed away during winter. As soon as they observed serviceberry trees blooming in the spring woodlands and roadside thickets, they began to anticipate the arrival of a preacher and planned "services" for their loved ones. Today, the United States Phenology Network recommends this tree to their citizen science partners tracking the arrival of spring. Native Americans used an infusion of serviceberry bark as a disinfectant and for bathing children with worms. The tasty berries were mashed, dried, and formed into little cakes and stored for winter. The tree's wood was used to craft arrows. If you can beat the birds to them, the berries can be used much like blueberries in muffins, jams, pies, or salads. Foragers sometimes dry the berries and add them to trail mixes.

Wild Friends

Native bees collect the pollen and nectar from the serviceberries' shaggy white flowers in early spring to make wee loafs of "bee bread" to feed newly hatching bees. Honeybees also use this plant as an early spring nectar and pollen source. Orioles, cardinals, robins, catbirds, and Eastern bluebirds love the berries of this small tree.

Wild grape

—

Vitis riparia

This is a long-lived, deciduous, perennial vine with a vigorous root system and large heart-shaped leaves with jagged edges. Fragrant, tiny, narrow, white spring flowers are followed by snazzy small dark purple clusters of tasty fruit.

ADDITIONAL COMMON NAMES:
riverbank grape, frost grape

NATIVE RANGE:
Eastern and central North America

HEIGHT:
up to 75 feet

SPREAD:
Rambling

HARDINESS ZONES:
2 to 8

BLOOM TIME:
May to June

Preferred Habitat and Cultivation

Riverbank grape flourishes in full sun to light shade planted in moist to moderately dry sites with fertile loamy soil, but it will tolerate other soil types. Frost grape produces larger and more flavorful fruit if located in full sun. Grape vines are twiners; they wrap their stems and forked tendrils around a climbing structure so they need a support like wires or an arbor.

Uses in the Garden and Landscape

Properly sited, frost grape can play both an ornamental and functional role in the landscape or garden. Its vertical growth habit is useful for screening fences, and it's attractive cultivated as a backdrop for secluded outdoor spaces or covering a large trellis or pergola. Wild riverbank grape planted in native hedgerows offers excellent year-round cover for rabbits, songbirds, pheasants, and bobwhite quail. Useful for biological pest management as an insectary plant; Japanese beetles are drawn away from other garden plants to feed on its leaves. Keep in mind wild grape can damage trees and shrubs, so be sure to utilize this plant's aggressive behavior to your advantage.

Wild Grape Butter

Pick the wild grapes before the first light frost. Stem and wash them, then cover them with water in a large covered pot, and bring to boil. Simmer for 30 minutes or until their skins pop. Stir and mash the grapes as they cook. Pour off the grape juice to be sweetened with honey, and drink.

Sieve the remaining grape pulp to remove the seeds and purée. Add an equal measure of maple sugar or honey, blending all in an oven-safe pot. Bake in a preheated 325 degree F oven, stirring occasionally, for 3 hours. Seal in hot, sterilized jars. Applesauce and grape purée maybe combined to create another tasty butter variation.

Native Harvests, Recipes and Botanicals of the American Indian–Courtesy E. Barrie Kavasch

Special Notes

Native Americans used the berries fresh in season and dried them for winter use. The grapes can be used for jellies, preserves, beverages, and vinegar. The edible fresh leaves are added to dill pickles and used in culinary dishes. The strong vines are wonderful for crafting baskets, wreaths, and decorative folk art.

Wild Friends

Native bees and wasps are the most common pollinators of wild grape flowers. Excellent fall food for a variety of wildlife.

Eastern Red Cedar

Juniperus virginiana

Red cedar is a dense evergreen tree with a variable columnar, oval, or pyramidal forms. The aromatic green foliage ranges in color from olive to dark blue-green. A distinctive characteristic of this tree is the variation in its leaf forms. Newly emerging foliage is prickly and needle-shaped, while more mature foliage is flat and scalelike. Red cedar is dioecious, producing pollen cones and seedcones on separate trees. The female tree's frosty gray-green, berrylike cones provide an excellent winter and early spring food source for birds. Eastern red cedar is tough and adapts to a variety of extreme weather and soil conditions.

ADDITIONAL COMMON NAMES:
pencil cedar, aromatic cedar, red cedar, and juniper

NATIVE RANGE:
Eastern United States

HEIGHT:
30 to 50 feet

SPREAD:
8 to 20 feet

HARDINESS ZONES:
2 to 9

BLOOM TIME:
Inconspicuous

Preferred Habitat and Cultivation

Red cedar thrives in full sun in a variety of habitats including alkaline, dry, or windy sites. Red cedar is a tolerant, long-lived evergreen plant that's useful for difficult areas. It was planted during the drought in the Dust Bowl era in the 1930s to help prevent soil erosion in the Great Plains and Southwest. Spring is the best time to establish nursery-grown starts in the garden or landscape. Red cedar is drought- and salt-tolerant and benefits from an occasional pruning to remove damaged or dead parts.

Juniper Disinfectant

- Simmer a handful fresh cedar needles and small stems in 2 cups of water for 20 to 30 minutes.

- Strain and pour the infused liquid into a small spray bottle.

- Add a squirt of liquid soap and 5 drops each of lavender, tea tree, and thyme essential oils.

- Shake well before each use.

- Use to disinfect hard surfaces.

Uses in the Garden and Landscape

Red cedar's aromatic evergreen foliage is useful for creating privacy screening and muting urban noise. It's attractive when used as a backdrop for other plantings in shared neighborhood and community landscapes. This evergreen shines when planted in naturalistic or wild settings and allowed to grow freely. Red Cedar is a low-maintenance tree and is widely used in shelter belts and wildlife plantings. Legends and superstitions surrounding the juniper tree date back to ancient times so it's a great specimen and story tree for children gardens or play areas. It's a worthy alternative evergreen to the Austrian pine and the invasive Japanese yew in the home landscape.

Special Notes

Cedar heartwood was once the main source of wood for pencils. Native Americans used the tree for building furniture and wigwams. The red aromatic heartwood was used to make love flutes and hunting bows. Cedar boughs were put on teepee poles to ward off lightning. For centuries, the berries, leaves, and twigs have been used in medicine and for flavoring food and beverages. The oil from juniper berries is considered "energizing" and is a popular ingredient in aromatherapy blends.

Wild Friends

Juniper has long been known in folklore as the tree of sanctuary for it offers safe haven for small animals and birds seeking shelter from predators. It is a favorite tree of Saint Francis, the patron saint of ecology and animals. Cedar waxwings, robins, bluebirds, turkeys, pheasants, and other fruit-eating birds love the berries. In addition to its berries, red cedar provides valuable protective and nesting cover for sparrows and cardinals within its dense foliage. It is the host plant for the caterpillar of the Olive Hairstreak butterfly.

The herb becomes the teacher. Men stray after false goals,while the herb he treads knows much, much more.
—Henry Vaughan

19th century artist lampoons the superstitions about how
epidemics spread and the use of herbal remedies. Wrapped up
on her herbs, she is safe from the cholera. Garlic bulb earrings,
bottles of herbal potions in her basket, aromatic herbs adorn her
skirt, and the windmill on her hat blows away evil air.

Harvesting and Preserving Herbs

A plant's lifecycle and time of year, along with the type of plant you are harvesting, will guide you to determine what parts to harvest and preserve.

Before consuming any plant gathered from the wild, make absolutely sure that you have correctly identified it. Beginners should only gather plants positively identified by a trained forager. To avoid contamination from car exhaust and other pollutants, plants should be harvested at least 100 feet from the nearest roadside or highway. City lots, urban fields, and lawns may have been sprayed with herbicides, pesticides or fertilizers. Do not eat any plant unless you are confident it is free from chemicals.

WHEN TO HARVEST

Harvesting can begin anytime there is sufficient foliage on the plant to tolerate cutting. Except for annuals at the end of their season, never cut back a plant completely when harvesting.

Rules of Thumb for Harvesting
- Harvest herbs in the morning after any dew has dried and before the sun gets too hot.
- Pick healthy growth and discard damaged flowers and leaves.
- Only harvest what you have time to prepare and use.
- Wash, dry, and preserve herbs as quickly as possible harvesting them.

When to Harvest Different Parts of a Plant

- Harvest leaves from herbs grown for their flavorful leaves just before the plant flowers.
- Harvest flowers for drying before they are fully open.
- Harvest root crops in fall when the plant parts are beginning to wither and dry. When harvesting roots, carefully dig and cut apart what you need; then replant the remainder of the root.
- Harvest seeds when they are fully ripened. You can cut the whole plant or just the seed stalk.

Soak all wild harvested greens for 20 minutes in a gallon of cold water combined with 3 tablespoons of vinegar or salt. Soaking will remove the dirt, insects, and other wild things clinging to the greens. When the greens have finished soaking, gently wash and rinse them in fresh water.

Ponder Your Possibilities!

Herbs for Pleasure & Purpose

- Flavoring culinary creations
- Decorative uses
- Aromatherapy
- Home pharmacy
- Brews, beverages & teas
- Native wisdom
- Cultural significance
- Edible flowers
- Gardening for wildlife
- Horticultural therapy
- Symbolism and rituals
- Companion planting
- Camouflage gardening

Air Drying Herbs

- Tie large leafy-stemmed herbs into loose bundles and hang them in a room or closet with good air circulation. It can take from two days to several weeks for the herbs to completely dry.
- Strip the fresh leaves or flowers from the plant stems and spread them in a thin layer on screens. You can use a house window screen lined with cheesecloth or paper towels. Place screens in a well-ventilated area to dry. Stir herbs several times a day to speed drying times.
- Hang plants harvested for seeds upside down to dry with the flowers/seedheads enclosed in paper bags to catch the dropping seeds.
- Thoroughly wash and scrub herb roots to remove the dirt. Split or slice large roots and spread in thin layers on drying screens in the open air.

Store dried herbs in clean glass jars away from the heat and light to preserve their flavors and fragrances.

Herb Vinegars

Unblemished, clean, dry herb leaves, seeds, roots, and flowers can all be utilized in vinegars, depending on the recipe. Use a high quality vinegar within an acidity level no lower than 5%. Place the herb parts in a clear glass container, pour the vinegar over them, tightly close the container, and let the container set for several weeks. At the end of the steeping time, strain herbs from the vinegar, and rebottle.

Basic Herb Butters

Combine 2 or 3 tablespoons of finely chopped herbs with 1 cup softened, unsalted butter. Some cooks like to add a tablespoon of olive oil to give the herb-butter mixture a more spreadable texture. You can add a pinch of salt dissolved in a bit of lemon juice also. Pack the butter into a small crock or form it into a log for slicing. Herb butters can be stored in a freezer for up to three months.

Freezing Fresh Herbs

There are three main ways to preserve herbs by freezing them.

- Carefully chop fresh-cut herbs with a knife, kitchen shears, or a food processor. Evenly spread the herbs on a baking sheet and freeze overnight. Pack the frozen herbs into small containers for later use.
- Freezing herbs in stock or water works well for preserving herbs for use in soups, stews, and dishes with a high water content. Place finely chopped herbs in broth or water, in the desired degree of concentration, and freeze in ice-cube trays. Remove the frozen cubes from the trays and store in containers or Ziploc-type bags. You can freeze edible flowers whole by placing them in ice cube trays; they're great added to drinks.
- To freeze herbs in oil, blend two cups of fresh, finely chopped herbs into one-half cup of good-quality oil. The oil acts as a carrier for the herbs, so use just enough oil to bind the mixture together. Pack the herbs into small containers and freeze for up to a year. Chip or scrape off what is needed. Herbs frozen in oil must be kept frozen until use.

References

Kingsbury Noel, (2014), *Gardening with Perennials*, The University of Chicago Press, Chicago and London, p.30

McDonough Cayte, (2015), *This Place We Call Home* | Ecological Landscape Alliance, http://www.ecolandscaping.org/09/native-plants/this-place-we-call-home/ (accessed February 25, 2017)

"Weed or Jet Fuel?" *Countryside & Small Stock Journal* Volume 101, Number 1 January/February 2017, p.26

Strauss Jenifer, Personal Native Process-Turning Points www.storybetold/turningpointd.htlm

Grand Traverse Stewardship Initiative, 2005

"Bumblebees? The Essential, Indefatigable Pollinators" www.bbg.org/gardening/article/bumble-bees_the_essential_indefatigable_poll (accessed January 19, 2017)

Quinn, Vernon, (1936), *Seeds: Their Place in Life and Legend*, Fredrick A. Stocks Company, USA

WEB RESOURCES

Invasive Species
Plant Conservation Alliance, Center for Invasive Species, Invasive Plant Atlas

The GreenBridges™ Initiative, The Herb Society of America
A program for gardeners interested in native herb conservation and discovering ways to incorporate native herbs into their yards and neighborhoods. Invasive plants, ecosystem function, and

reputable sources for native herbs are among the key concepts covered in program materials. www.herbsociety.org

Ecosystem Services Fact Sheets
Fact sheets developed for public dissemination on the general topics of ecosystem services and one for each service covered in the Tool Kits. The fact sheets can be downloaded and distributed at local gardening events. www.esa.org/ecoservices/comm/body. comm.fact.ecos.html.

Action Bioscience Ecosystem Services: A Primer
Ecological Society of America www.actionbioscience.org

Ask Nature Biomimicry is an approach to innovation that seeks sustainable solutions to human challenges by emulating nature's time-tested patterns and strategies. Their goal is to create products, processes, and policies—new ways of living—that are well-adapted to life on earth over the long haul. www.Asknature. org.

Gardener's Supply Company, Burlington Vermont
Build Your Own Rain Garden, Perennial Garden Design Sheet #1. www.gardeners.com

Pollinator Partnership/North American Pollinator Protection Campaign
Information for gardeners, educators, and resource managers to encourage the health of resident and migratory pollinator animals. Extensive planting references & resources based on Bailey's Ecoregions of the United States. www.pollinator.org

Bug Guide
An online resource devoted to insect, spiders and their kin, with identification help and information. For the United States and Canada. www.bugguide.net

Ecological Landscape Alliance

Discover ecological landscaping [2005 Brochure]. Retrieved September 21, 2016 from www.ecolandscaping.org/wp-content/uploads/2011/05/Discover-Ecological-Landscaping-Brochure.pdf.

Bee-Friendly with Winnie-the Pooh

The British Beekeepers Association with Egmont Publishing, in 2015, created this special Bee-Freindly Guide (PDF) for families inspired by Winnie-the-Pooh and Friends. Filled with fun upbeat educational materials: http://friendofthehoneybee.com

Xerces Society for Invertebrate Conservation

International nonprofit organization that protects wildlife through the conservation of invertebrates and their habitat. Provide speakers and resources for garden clubs and Master Gardening groups. www.xerces.org

USDA Plant hardiness Zone Map

Available online at http://planthardiness.ars.usda.gov/PHZMWeb/#
Knowing the lowest average temperature a plant is likely to experience is the first thing to consider when selecting plants. "Careless culture" exposure to sun, wind, moisture, and salt often kills more plants than cold temperatures

Pat Crocker

Culinary Herbalist, Food and garden photographer
Lively, timely, and entertaining, Pat Crocker brings her extensive food and herb expertise to the podium every time she speaks. A professional Home Economist, writer and author, Pat's presentations and demonstrations are infused with the joy of using the "helping plants" in everyday life.
Blog: Pat Crocker: patcrocker.com

Debra Knapke The Garden Sage

Garden designer, lecturer, teacher, and advisor" describe Debra's work. Located in central Ohio, she shares her work throughout the midwest and is an often requested speaker at garden clubs, horticulture related events, book fairs, libraries and non-profit organizations.

Blog: Heartland Gardening debrathegardensage.com

Citizen Science & Phenology

Habitat Network

Developed by Cornell Lab and powered by YardMap, Habitat Network is a citizen science project designed to help you work together with your neighbors to create nature-friendly regional landscapes. One of the best citizen science projects in the United States. Extensive ecoregion planting references and resources. www.yardmap.org or email help@habitat.network

Plant Watch

www.plantwatch.ca

Project BudBurst, Timing Is Everything

www.budbust.org

Natures Calendar

www.naturescalendar.org.uk

Backyard Nature

www.backyardnature.net

Four Directions Teachings Department of Canadian Heritage http://www.fourdirectionsteachings.com/

Blanchan, Neltje (1907). *Nature's Garden*, Doubleday, Page & Company, New York, NY

Bown, D. (1995). *Encyclopedia of Herbs and their Uses*, Dorling Kindersley, New York, NY

Burrell, Colston C. (2006) *Native Alternatives to Invasive Plants: Brooklyn Botanic Garden All Regions Guide*, Brooklyn BotanicGarden Inc., New York, NY

Cloyd, Raymond A., Nixon, Philip L., & Pataky, Nancy R. (2001). *IPM for Gardeners, A Guide to Integrated Pest Management*, Timber Press, Portland, OR

Darke, Rick & Tallamy, W. Douglas (2014). *The Living Landscape: Designing for Beauty and Biodiversity in the Home Garden*, Timber Press, Portland, OR

Dickinson, Janis L. & Bonny, Rick (2012). *Citizen Science Public Participation in Environmental Research*, Comstock Publishing Associates, Ithaca, NY & London

Gips, Kathleen (1990). Flora's Dictionary, *The Victorian Language of Herbs and Flowers*, TMPublications, Chargrin Falls, Ohio

Gibbs, Jay, Bennett, Ashley, Isaacs, R. & Landis, J. (2015) *Bees of the Great Lakes Region and Wildflowers to Support Them*, Michigan State University Extension Bulletin E3282

Gray, Beverly (2011) *The Boreal Herbal: Wild Food and Medicine Plants of the North: Guide to Harvesting, Preserving and Preparing*, Aroma Borealis Press, Canada

Griffin, Brian L. (1997). *Humbleblebee-Bumblebee*, Knox Cellers, Bellingham, WA

Heiser, Charles B. (2003). *Weeds in My Garden-Observations on Some Misunderstood Plants*, Timber Press, Portland, OR

Kavasch, Barrie (1977). *Native Harvests, Recipes and Botanicals of the American Indian*, Random House, New York, NY

Keeler, Harriet L. (1923). *Our Native Trees*, Charles Scribner's Sons, New York, NY

Lehane, Brendan (1997). *The Power of Plants*, McGraw-Hill Co. UK Ltd., London, England

Leslie, Clare Walker & Roth, Charles E. (1996). *Nature Journaling: Learning to Observe and Connect with the World around You*, Storey Communications, Adams, MA

Lewis, C.A. (1996). *Green Nature/Human Nature: The Meaning of Plants in our Lives*, University of Illinois Press, Urbana, IL

Loewer, Peter (1996). *Thoreau's Garden: Native Plants for the American Landscape*, Stackpole Books, Mechanicsburg, PA

Moerman, Daniel E. (1998). *Native American Ethnobotany*, Timber Press, Portland, OR, London

Rainer, Thomas & West, Claudia (2015). *Planting in a Post-Wild World: Designing Plant Communities for Resilient Landscapes*, Timber Press, Portland, OR

Sanders, Jack (2003). *The Secrets of Wildflowers: A Delightful Feast of Little-known Facts, Folklore and History*, Globe Pequot Press, Guilford, CT

Stokes, Donald & Lillian (1984). *Stokes Nature Guides: Enjoying Wild Flowers*, Little, Brown, and Company, New York, NY

Tallamy, W. Douglas (2007). *Bringing Nature Home, How You Can Sustain Wildlife with Native Plants*, Timber Press, Portland, OR

Watts, May Theilgaard (1974). *Reading The Landscape*, Macmillan Publishing, New York, NY

Wilder, Louise B. (1974). *The Fragrant Garden, A Book About Sweet Scented Flowers and Leaves*, Dover Publications Inc., New York, NY

Wilkins, Malcome (1988). *PlantWatching: How Plants Remember, Tell Time, Form Relationships and More*, Facts on File Inc., New York, NY

Photo & Recipe Credits

JERIE ARTZ
Jeri Artz painted the beautiful watercolor for the cover of this book.

PAT CROCKER
Pat Crocker is a culinary herbalist and food and garden photographer.
Blog: patcrocker.com
Photos:
Wild Ginger leaf and flower
Witch Hazel leaf & stem
Violet

E. BARRIE KAVASCH
E. Barrie Kavasch is a herbalist, ethnobotanist, mycologist, and food historian of Cherokee, Creek, and Powhatan descent, with Scotch-Irish, English, and German heritage as well. She is the author of two books on Native American foods, *Enduring Harvests* (1995, Globe Pequot) and *Native Harvests* (1979, Random House), which was hailed by *The New York Times* as "the most intelligent and brilliantly researched book on the foods of the American Indians."

Native Harvests, Recipes and Botanicals of the American Indian
Recipes:
Indian Pudding
Wild Grape Butter
Garlic Mustard Sauce
Wild Bergamot Tea
Goldenrod Tea

DEBRA KNAPKE
Debra Knapke is a garden designer, lecturer, teacher, and author. Located in central Ohio, she shares her work throughout the Midwest and is an often requested speaker at garden clubs, horticulture-related events, book fairs, libraries, and nonprofit organizations.

Blog: Heartland Gardening at DebraTheGardenSage.com
Photo:
Iris cristata

KATHERINE SCHLOSSER
Author, advisor, and The Herb Society of America Native Plant
Committee Chair
Photo:
Spicebush flower
Recipe:
Indian Lemonade

ROBERTA SMITH
Roberta Smith is a Chaska, Minnesota Master Gardener.
Photos:
Rain barrel
Thyme lawn

GUDRUN WITTGEN
Silhouette paper cutouts, Scherenschnitt
Gudrun Wittgen is a member of the Guild of American
Papercutters. She has been featured in newspaper and magazine
articles and interviewed for television specials. Her work is
exhibited in numerous galleries and museums, and she has received
various awards. She counts art and humane societies among her
favorite causes.

Additional Photo Credits
Bearberry, Wikimedia commons Jesse Taylor
Barren strawberry, Wikimedia commons Melissa McMasters
Grindelia Squarrosa, Wikimedia Commons
Witch hazel flower, Wikimedia commons AnRo0002
Elderberry flower, Wikimedia commons
Bloodroot, Wikimedia commons
Sumac, Wikimedia commons

All other photos credit to the author

Meet Susan Betz

Susan Betz is an author, garden communicator, lecturer, and conservationist specializing in herbs and native plants. She is a charter member and past president of the Michigan Herb Associates. She has been actively involved in promoting gardening with herbs for over 35 years. Susan is a member of the International Herb Association, Garden Writers Association, and the Ecological Landscape Alliance. A life member of The Herb Society of America, Susan serves on HSA's Native Herb Conservation committee and the GreenBridges™ committee, the Herb Society's sustainable garden initiative. Susan is the author of the book *Magical Moons & Seasonal Circles Stop-Look-Listen Stepping into the Circle of the Seasons*. She lives and gardens in Jonesville, Michigan, with her husband David and beloved dogs Pike, Emma Graber, and Ginger.

CPSIA information can be obtained
at www.ICGtesting.com
Printed in the USA
BVHW02s1508290418
513941BV00027B/124/P